Imus,
Mike and the Mad Dog,
& Doris from Rego Park

Imus,
Mike and the Mad Dog,
& Doris from Rego Park

THE GROUNDBREAKING
HISTORY OF WFAN

Tim Sullivan

TRIUMPH
B O O K S

Library of Congress Cataloging-in-Publication Data
Sullivan, Tim, 1972-
   Imus, Mike and The Mad Dog & Doris from Rego Park : the groundbreaking history of WFAN / Tim Sullivan.
      pages cm
      ISBN 978-1-60078-828-4
      1. Radio broadcasting of sports—New York (State)—New York— History. 2. WFAN (Radio station: New York, N.Y.)—History. 3. Radio broadcasters—United States—Biography. I. Title. II. Title: Imus, Mike and The Mad Dog, and Doris from Rego Park.
      GV742.3.S85 2013
      070.449796—dc23   2013027585

This book is available in quantity at special discounts for your group or organization. For further information, contact:
   Triumph Books LLC
   814 North Franklin Street
   Chicago, Illinois 60610
   (312) 337-0747
   www.triumphbooks.com

Printed in U.S.A.
ISBN: 978-1-60078-828-4
Design by Sue Knopf

In loving memory of Carol A. Smyth,
looking down on us all, always.
Thank you for the inspiration and motivation.

Contents

Foreword

ANYBODY WHO DECIDES TO WRITE A BOOK about WFAN is writing a book about the knowledge, the passion, and the energy of the New York sports fan—a passion and energy that many times exceeds the passion and energy of the players and teams that they root for. The ones that they watch every day, the ones that they live and die for.

WFAN has become a part of daily life for the New York sports fan, a part of their DNA, their lifestyle. It is a place where they can speak of the unspeakable, and express what's to see from sometimes the unwatchable.

WFAN has become the stoop in the neighborhood, the office watercooler. It's you and your radio, and it's always there for you, in good times and bad, as long as you have a radio nearby.

WFAN is underneath the streetlamp; it is those two stools that are there at your favorite bar, or anywhere fans can sit or stand to schmooze the sports of New York whenever they so choose.

Fans have always done so in this great city, of course. They've always found places to connect with each other and talk sports. But for the last 26-plus years, they've also been able to broadcast it to the masses on this great station. They've been able to talk, listen, and absorb all of New York sports which, to so many of them, is all that matters.

WFAN has made the connection with the city, with the fans, with the people. And it is a connection that will never be broken. After all, it is a radio station for the people, a radio station that is family and is as intimate and as personal as you can be with a substantial number of New Yorkers listening every day.

If WFAN is a part of your life, it is safe to say that this book is a must-read, especially when so much of it is about you and the teams we care about. This is a book about WFAN, about New York, about sports, but most of all, about you and the station you love to listen to.

—*Steve Somers*

1

New York, New York

We were having fun. The very first day I wrote an opening manifesto, and basically what I said was, this was a medium that was going to change the universe. People were going to quit their jobs to stay home and listen to us. People were going to sit on hold for hours and hours and hours waiting to be put on the air so they can say "The Mets suck." And all of the things that I predicted—facetiously of course—turned out to be true. It was a whimsical look at what might happen with sports radio. And, of course, it all happened.   —JIM LAMPLEY

ED COLEMAN HAD HEARD IT ALL BEFORE. This concept of a 24-hours-a-day sports radio station that was going to change the world. Constant talk, constant news, constant interaction about the games people play. A bar without the alcohol, a clubhouse without the lockers, a psychiatrist's office without the couch. Call it what you will. It was to be a place for sports fans to talk, well, sports at any point in the day.

What a novel idea.

But you can excuse Coleman for not jumping for joy when he first caught wind of a New York operation plotting out this move in 1986. After all, he had lived through it already...and it didn't turn out so well. To steal a New York sports line from the unmistakable, unforgettable Yogi Berra, it was déjà vu all over again for the man known as Eddie C.

Coleman, a radio host and graduate of the famed Syracuse University S.I. Newhouse School of Public Communications, was busy in the 1980s carving out an identity in a tough business in his native Boston. He was living the dream and hoping for more when a colleague named John Chanin gave him a call that changed his life.

Chanin was a topflight radio executive who had cut his teeth as the sports director and executive producer at ABC Radio Sports and held many trailblazing roles before his death in 2006. He clearly was the right guy to be tasked with making sports radio a reality for an outfit called Enterprise Radio at the turn of the decade.

"It was something of a precursor to ESPN Radio, and John had called me, probably sometime in 1980, and wondered if I would be interested in coming down," Coleman said. "I had a pretty good job at that point at WBZ [AM 1030] in Boston. But my boss really wasn't going anywhere and I had nowhere to go at the station but to do what I had been doing."

Enterprise was a concept driven by Scott Rasmussen of the soon-to-be-famous ESPN Rasmussens. Scott's father, Bill, created the Entertainment Sports and Programming Network, and Scott set out to create the radio version of the television channel with the household name. Along the way, he made no bones about playing a copycat role to the television network that would eventually label itself "The Worldwide Leader in Sports." Enterprise, after all, set up shop in Avon, Connecticut, some 15 miles away from ESPN's headquarters in Bristol, and, like ESPN, wanted to hire names from major markets and install them in a little slice of suburban New England tucked neatly away in Hartford County.

Coleman, for one, was sold. He walked away from Beantown and his post at WBZ in January of 1981, and jumped at the opportunity to lay the foundation for this groundbreaking sports concept.

And who could blame him? It all seemed so perfect, right?

"I thought about it, and eventually I said, 'Sure, I'll come down,'" Coleman said with a reminiscent laugh. "'I'll take the chance.'"

By September, Coleman was out of a job and Enterprise had closed its doors.

"In the end, it was a little bit too early for it to take off," Coleman said. "We went out of business quickly, and long story short, some nine months later, I'm looking for work just like everyone else who went there."

Enterprise didn't attract the advertising dollars it needed to stay afloat. After all, the studio—with all of its equipment—wasn't cheap. And neither were the paychecks it had to sign for the talent that filled those entrepreneurial airwaves. Less than a year after this can't-miss project was launched, it missed.

But Chanin, as all good executives do, kept a file on his skill people. Did he feel bad that Enterprise flopped? Sure. Did he want to make it up to some of the personalities somewhere down the line, talent that dropped everything and moved to the middle of Nowheresville, Connecticut? Absolutely.

For Coleman—and for all of sports radio for that matter—that opportunity came six years later. And that second time, indeed, was a charm.

In 1986, another radio dreamer took a crack at changing the world, and he had the money to back it up. Jeff Smulyan of Emmis Communications, an Indianapolis-based radio enterprise, purchased a dying AM country music station—in New York City of all places —for $10 million, and pledged to turn it into a 24-hour all-sports radio station. WHN 1050 was the New York home of Kenny Rogers, Willie Nelson, and Dolly Parton, but it was also the flagship station of the defending-world-champion New York Mets, which Smulyan thought was a decent launching pad, if nothing else.

"It was something I always wanted to do, and I had thought about it years and years before when I was in college in the late 1960s. I was always kind of a radio junkie. That was the very beginning of all-news radio and I really thought about it for sports. I thought it could work," Smulyan said. "It was one of those things I always kept tucked away in the back of my mind. So, I was in New York one night and I started talking about it with others. I wanted to do it simply because we knew—going back to those days, in the mid-1980s—that FM was great for certain types of music—rock 'n' roll, beautiful music, Top 40—but the thought was country wouldn't make the transition."

Especially in New York, right?

"Right. And the prevailing wisdom was that WHN, at the time, was the largest country music station in America. But in New York, it was probably ranked 20th," Smulyan said. "So, from our standpoint, we didn't think it was *that* spectacular. We felt we could change it up."

Smulyan didn't rise up the corporate ladder without the ability to make smart decisions. And while the sports concept seemed risky—bordering on crazy, even—he was clearly smart enough to know he needed a seasoned leader to steer the ship. Someone who'd been through it all before, someone who might have learned from past mistakes.

Enter Chanin...again.

"What we had was a radio station which we thought was going to be an also-ran in the country music world, and we thought New York didn't have a great affinity for country, obviously, anyway,"

Smulyan said. "And in that same radio station, it was half Major League Baseball because it had the Mets. That was important.

"The theory, for us, was if the AM band is only going to be information, and you had WINS [1010] and WCBS [880] doing news, and you had WWOR [710] and WABC [770] doing talk. It was pretty clear you weren't going to do news or talk and stand out. So, we thought our theory was a great chance to do all sports, and I used to refer to it as the shopping center analogy. You had an anchor tenant in the Mets, and for baseball that means you have 180 days a year where you're going to attract sufficient listeners to the radio station. So, we start from there, we grow out, and we see where that takes us.

"That was the thesis."

But, boy, was it a tough sell. Before Smulyan could even get the concept out of the conference room and onto the airwaves, there were layers upon layers of opposition.

"We had a managers meeting, and I'll never forget it. Steve Crane, one of the founders of Emmis and one of my oldest friends, loved it. I loved the idea, as well, obviously, and [then–sales director of Emmis] Joel Hollander loved the idea, too. But most of our managers thought we were nuts. Nuts," Smulyan said. "You have to know Emmis to know that it is sort of a very collaborative venture. So we had a managers meeting and took a vote on the idea…and it failed.

"I'll never forget, we walked out of the meeting and Steve asked, 'What do you want to do?' I said, 'You can't lead where no one will follow, so we're not going to do all sports. We're just not.'"

This underdog concept, though, picked itself right up off the mat less than 24 hours later, somehow. And the rest is history.

The Rocky of radio.

"The next day," Smulyan said, as his voice picked up in volume and enthusiasm, "Rick Cummings, who was then and is now the head of programming for this company, came in and said, 'Well, we think it's a stupid idea. Stupid. But we owe you one. So, let's go ahead and do it.'"

And just like that, sports radio—in its second at-bat overall and first in New York—was off and running. A station that would soon change its call letters to WFAN and be known globally as The Fan, was finally more than just a dream on the AM dial.

"The key is that we had to find someone to run the station, because frankly we didn't want to be *that* involved in it," Smulyan said. "We found a guy named John Chanin who was our first program director, and whose wife gave the station the name, The Fan. John's tenure there wasn't wonderful and John passed away many years ago, but he was the one who got it off the ground."

It wasn't easy, and there were certainly plenty of early errors to go with the hits. Chanin, for starters, was still in that ABC/ESPN/national/international mind-set. He set out to attract national names, and not necessarily New Yorkers, for the on-air positions.

That was Mistake No. 1.

"It was a debatable theory. I think John's original vision was to make it more of a network concept, and we all felt it had to be more local," Smulyan said. "When we hired people, sure, a lot of people thought we were nuts. On the other hand, some people were intrigued."

If nothing else, the names Chanin hired drew headlines. People knew them, and it made for some pre-air buzz, which certainly helped the cause for WFAN.

Greg Gumbel, who would eventually rise to stardom calling NFL games for CBS Sports, was hired as the morning host. He was a part of the New York media at the time, but he was not a New Yorker, and there is a big, big difference. But Gumbel came in with MSG Network and ESPN on his resume, and he fit the early bill for WFAN. He was marketable. He was a name.

"Greg's agent and Greg liked the idea," Smulyan said. "We knew that mornings would be very tough in New York, but Greg did it."

Jim Lampley was next. An icon in the sports broadcasting world who had worked for ABC Sports, would eventually move on to NBC Sports as well as CBS Sports, and now is the ever-present, eloquent, and smiling face of HBO Sports, Lampley, it seemed, could bring experience and knowledge to the table, all with a hint of humor and a real-world charm that would help make the station stand out.

"We entered into contract negotiations, discussions, and I ultimately agreed to do it. The irony was I'm pretty certain the big reason they wanted me was my identity with ABC Sports," Lampley said. "I'd been at ABC Sports for 13 years. I'd been the host for college football for six or seven years and had gotten into the studio for the Olympics and things like that. So I had a national image and reputation. I think that the management of the station thought that, given that it was the New York market, that it would be useful to have people like that. That accounted for me and that accounted for Greg Gumbel at the beginning."

"When he was hired," Smulyan said of Lampley, "he seemed like a perfect fit for what we wanted to do with the midday show."

And to carry the afternoon drive time after Lampley—the most important part of the radio day in New York—Chanin and company tabbed Pete Franklin, a shock jock in Ohio who made headlines for his loud-and-proud opinions and his have-no-fear approach to just about anything he did.

"Ahh yes, Pete," Smulyan said. "He was a name, too, and we brought him to see what he could do."

Other names would follow. Coleman, who came around to the idea of All-Sports Radio, Act 2, despite the failure of Act 1, was one of them. He had trekked back to Boston—proverbial tail between his legs and all—after the Enterprise demise, and regained a position at WBZ. But he had always been intrigued by the idea of New York radio. Burned once by the concept, there was something that kept drawing him back to the possibilities.

"So there I am, back at WBZ, and John called again. I guess it was early 1986," Coleman said. "And he said, 'I'm forming an all-sports station.' All I could say was, 'Okay, this sounds really familiar, John.'

"But the last time, with Enterprise, it was a supposed network. Wasn't going to work. This was a station in New York City, and he said, 'I think I might be able to make this work.' So I took a chance again and went down. The rest is history.

"In the back of my mind, though, there was always the thought that I'd be back in Boston after a couple of years."

Skepticism wasn't Coleman's alone. Everyone on this maiden voyage—where mistakes were plentiful on and off the air—had some doubts about the long-term prospects of the station, even Smulyan.

"There was a lot of thought to kill it off before it took off," he said. "We were fortunate the company had the staying power to stick with it."

And so with names like Gumbel, Lampley, Coleman, Suzyn Waldman, and Howie Rose in tow, WFAN launched on July 1, 1987, at 3:00 PM. After a quick bumper intro, the first voice to be heard that day was Waldman's, who gave a top-of-the-hour sports update leading into Lampley's show.

"*Sports Radio 1050. W-F-A-N. New York City,*" the intro bellowed. "*All Sports. All The Time.*"

"Good afternoon, everybody, and welcome to the first broadcast of WFAN, All Sports, 1050. You're sharing a part of radio history with us today," Waldman proclaimed. "This is the beginning of the first 24-hour-a-day sports station. I'm Suzyn Waldman. The message board outside Yankee Stadium today reads VINTAGE GUIDRY, and last night was indeed a classic Gator performance. Guidry struck out nine and only walked one as the Yanks extended their lead to two games in the AL East."

Like an expansion team feeling its way through its inaugural season, there were plenty of bumps in the road for Waldman and Co. in those early days. And unlike so many expansion teams these days that get to begin life in spanking-new stadiums and ballparks, WFAN did not operate out of a gem of a building. Not even close.

The famed Kaufman Astoria Studios in Queens had plenty of charm and history and elegance. How could they not? It was, after all, a movie studio that hosted the first two films made by the Marx brothers—*The Cocoanuts* and *Animal Crackers*—and much later in its esteemed life would add *Goodfellas* and *Carlito's Way* to its ledger.

Photos of famous entertainers who passed through the famed establishment line the halls. Clearly, nostalgia oozes out of the joint.

In the bowels of the place, however, other stuff oozes out.

"If you loved history, this was your place," said Don La Greca, an update anchor who later joined The Fan's ranks. "I mean, the Marx brothers worked there! But, keep in mind, WFAN was situated in the basement of the place. The basement."

Indeed, if The Fan was to rattle the radio world and turn it on its ear, it was going to have to do it in a ramshackle box, pushed way below all the glory resonating upstairs. This is a studio that just about everyone who called it home at some point in their careers remembers.

And not for the right reasons.

"What a pit," Coleman said with a laugh. "What an absolute armpit. It was unbelievable. Here you are, in this historic building that used to do Marx brothers movies in there. That was pretty much the soundstage for Hollywood before there was Hollywood! So, you go way back, and it was a great, great building.

"But the basement? Different story. I never saw the rats running around, but I'm sure they were there. There were no windows, no nothing. The newsroom was...manageable, let's put it that way.

"I remember the first time I walked in there. It was like, 'So this is what I've come to, huh? Great!' I left a pretty good gig in Boston at a pretty good station, and there I was, sitting in a basement in Astoria, Queens."

Cracks in the foundation. Stains on the wall. Dust stalactites hanging from the ceiling. A musty smell—to put it mildly—surrounded the place. You name it, this studio had it.

"The actual radio station itself was, no, not cutting edge at all," said Jody McDonald, another original who would eventually wear several hats at WFAN, including midday talk show host. "Not state of the art. Rather old and decrepit more than anything else. But what's funny is when I first started there, I had no idea! Having never worked in professional radio before, I just had no idea. It took me time to figure out that, 'Man, as big of a radio station as this is, and as popular as we've become, this place really should be a heck of a lot better.'"

Ian Eagle—a New Yorker born and bred to be in the radio business, complete with the uncanny ability to get his point across with as few words and as much wit as possible—was busy getting his broadcasting degree at Syracuse when The Fan launched. But he would make it there soon enough and will never forget his memories of what he faithfully refers to bluntly, as "a complete shithole" of a studio.

"Not good," Eagle said, as only he can. "Just...not good. I've been out of the place for years, and I'm still feeling flu-like symptoms."

Rose, who came over from WHN, where he served as sports director, would soon be on his way to beginning one of the most impressive play-by-play careers in sports broadcasting history. Like

McDonald, he was young, he was happy to be there, and let's face it, the amount of dust in the corner wasn't going to make a difference to him or his on-air product.

But to this day, what stands out for Rose is the quality of the station's equipment, or lack thereof.

"My biggest recollection was not so much, 'I can't believe we're here.' But my impression back then was of constantly thinking, *I can't believe we got through a show without getting knocked off the air!* I mean, the first couple of months there were technical problems daily. Sometimes hourly," he said with a laugh. "That's not necessarily a reflection of any individual who worked there, but I think the enormity of what we were doing from a technical standpoint, in terms of taking phone calls all day and all night and doing remotes—that was the type of stuff that hadn't been done the way we were doing it...ever.

"So that didn't only create creative challenges, but it created technical ones. And man, we had our share of technical challenges."

There were plenty of logistical ones, as well. After all, it didn't take long for Chanin's national approach to grate on New Yorkers. The big names and voices that sat in front of WFAN microphones in the early days were recognizable and they could clearly work a room at a banquet.

But on radio? In New York? Fuhgeddaboudit.

You have to keep in mind that New Yorkers—especially sports fans in the five boroughs—aren't always keen on national sports subjects. Give them the Yankees and the Mets, give them the Giants and the Jets, and skip the boxing, the college football, and the NASCAR, thank you very much. It's a different place, and while the efforts of Gumbel and Lampley and Franklin were admirable, it just wasn't working.

"I'll never forget going to the press conference at Toots Shor's restaurant, which was not the original but another one that came along later near Madison Square Garden. And this is in May of '87," Rose recalled. "I think it was John Chanin, rather than Jeff Smulyan, who said, 'We are launching a nationwide talent search.' I thought to myself, *We're screwed. We don't need a nationwide talent search! We need a citywide talent search!*

"I just knew, inherently, the only way this was going to work was if we sounded like New York. As soon as I heard 'nationwide talent search,' I said, 'We're not going to sound like New York.' Because I don't care how big of a name you get, I don't care how successful he's been in another market, if he doesn't at least have New York roots, then he's going to misrepresent everything that is sacred to the people who are going to be listening and ultimately judging the future of this radio station! I don't think you needed to be particularly prophetic to have that mind-set. But I think the early returns would certainly support my thinking."

Especially in the morning. In hindsight, it shouldn't have come as a surprise. As any loyal NFL fan who tunes into CBS on fall Sundays can tell you, Gumbel is thorough, knowledgeable, and even emphatic, when needed, on his play-by-play calls.

But he's not all that funny. And he's not all that loud. In New York or elsewhere, that's what you need in morning radio, folks.

"Most people don't remember that our first morning man was Greg Gumbel," Smulyan said. "I always joke there are more people on this phone call than there were people listening to Greg in the first year."

Gumbel declined several requests to be interviewed for this book.

"Greg is a very, very professional, straightforward guy," Lampley said. "The kind of crazy stuff for radio, Greg would never do that. Greg is more down the middle and people love that about him. But he's purely an informational guy. He wasn't going to stretch and do crazy stuff on the air. At the end of the day, you have to feel like you're a New Yorker."

Gumbel was born in New Orleans.

"I don't want to put it all on his lap or anybody else's lap as an individual, but Greg doesn't have a New York background," Rose said. "There's only so far he can go before he would be somewhat exposed as either not knowing that Houston Street is pronounced How-ston Street and not Hew-ston Street, or not having lived through the down years the Jets had after the Super Bowl or all those bad years the Yankees had from '65 to '75. He didn't go through that.

"And ultimately, if you're doing a talk show, the beauty of it is you're not hanging up on one guy and picking up another call, you're sharing your life. It's an intimate medium to begin with. But a talk show takes that intimacy to a whole different level because if you're going to do it in the way I believe in doing it, you're putting everything about yourself out there, for the most part. You're not going to give them carte blanche about your life. But you're going to make a concerted effort to connect.

"And for me, I thought that would be easy because of having grown up here, and when I mentioned I went to P.S. 205 or Junior High School 74 or Cardozo High School [in Queens], somewhere along the line people know those schools. People know those neighborhoods. I would refer to guys I grew up with in the schoolyard— maybe one or two guys would have heard it live and rang up another one and said, 'Hey, he was talking about you!'

"That kind of stuff has tentacles, you know? It reaches out to where people say, 'Hey, maybe he's going to talk about where I went to school, or at the very least that we had a rivalry with that school.' Those are things that Greg Gumbel or Jim Lampley or anyone else who came from elsewhere could not possibly have been able to do. It might sound like a small thing but you have to be visionary about it and realize that you're growing a relationship and that relationship is predicated on background.

"I think that's very important to building intimacy within a talk show format."

Lampley, though, had fun along the way, and clearly delivered the charm that Chanin saw in him, win, lose, or draw. He built a rapport with some of the area callers, and even gave them assignments from time to time, because—quite frankly—he needed the help. Forget not being from New York; a few days into his gig, he wasn't even doing it from New York.

"I went to work and did that first show for WFAN on July 1, and on July 2, I went into the office at ABC and quit. That had not been part of the plan. I wound up in a circumstance where I went looking for other things to do in my television career, and by September, I had to leave New York to go to Los Angeles to work for CBS," Lampley recalled. "Since I was already doing the morning radio show, 10:00 AM to 1:00 PM at WFAN, I had established the identity and been on the air a couple months. I didn't want to change, didn't want to walk out on them because of my location.

"So, I wound up doing about a year of local radio on a New York radio station from a studio in Los Angeles! It was called the Hollywood Satellite Show. In those days, the Internet wasn't present, and I would get the information on what happened in New York sports the night before delivered in fax material the following morning."

But the faxes just weren't enough. For statistics, sure. For the play by play, absolutely. But to soak up the true culture of New York sports, to help fully illustrate what was going on in the Big Apple from one night to the next, he needed the aid of the callers.

"I got into it and I think—in a way—it was working. I was quite aware of the local focus and I elicited the listeners as my reporters in that regard," Lampley said. "So, I had various listeners who were loyal callers, of course, and they became my beat reporters. And as soon as I came on the air, doing the show from Hollywood, I would have my reporters on, and they'd give us all of the scoop.

"Sam from Bayonne—I will never forget Sam from Bayonne. Loyal caller. He would come on and tell me what happened with the Devils and the Rangers the night before. I had another caller who was the Mets reporter, another caller who was the Yankees reporter, and that made some of that fun."

But it clearly wasn't built to last. The ratings were small and the advertising dollars coming in to the station were smaller. And as innovative and creative and entrepreneurial as the whole WFAN concept was, obviously something had to turn soon or the project was going to turn into Enterprise Radio, Take 2.

"I can remember the first weekend, will never forget it, because I happened to be on vacation with my family in the Hamptons," Smulyan said. "I was listening and hearing an awful lot of commercials for do-it-yourself funerals! Over and over again.

"I started thinking, *Oh my God. I don't know how much they're paying us for that, but whatever it is, it's not enough.* I found out later that you don't get paid at all for them. That's what we were dealing with at the time. There weren't a lot of advertisers at the beginning of WFAN. Joel Hollander says one of the worst moments in his life was about six months into The Fan, and we were walking down the street in New York, and I turned to him and said, 'Jesus, Joel, can't you sell something to somebody?' Joel's one of the great salesmen in the history of this business, but it was tough early on for him and for all of us."

On-air guests might help the transition, the executives thought. More name power, more reason to listen, might mean more reasons to buy advertising time. Worth a shot, right? But like all else in the early stages, getting the right kind of star just to agree to an interview was a tall mountain to climb.

"Yeah, it was a process, and I think they had to learn how to do local shows," said Mike Francesa, another tried-and-true New Yorker who was at CBS Sports when WFAN launched. "They had to make the shows local in feel and find people who were New York hosts and find people who would appeal to the New York audience. That's how it was going to work."

McDonald, who had both a New York background, as he grew up there, as well as a national journalistic background, because he had worked at ESPN, was eager to jump into this guest procession and take his shot, even though he was on overnight duty and realized it'd be a chore to even find someone awake when he needed one.

Little did he know that in the process, he'd learn that The Fan needed to be what Rose and the others had clearly believed all along.

Local, local, local.

"We did a couple practice shows, which was good, to get used to it, but that first time you go behind the mic and you're talking to real people, it's a little on the terrifying side. It was for me, for sure, and we were hoping to get some guests early in the show," McDonald said. "We knew it would be difficult to book guests for 3:00 in the morning, and so we figured we'd start the show with guests. So my producer was a good guy by the name of Jim Memolo, who got behind the mic himself. He does the morning show on Sirius' baseball channel now. Jimmy was my first producer and he booked [tight end] Todd Christensen, who at the time was still playing for the Raiders.

"He was a former Giant and we thought the New York tie would be good. He was out in California, which helped, too, and it wasn't so bad to ask him to come on with the time change and all. And they were scheduled to play the Giants in a couple weeks and the Jets in a couple weeks, so that was good.

"We get Todd to come on, he agrees, I do my spiel, talk about the Mets—they lost that night—the Yankees, whatever else, but believe it or not football will be here soon. It was July and camps were almost opening. Todd Christensen, Raiders, a real, live, professional football player was a guest! I thought it was a pretty good get.

"So I get Christensen on and we do 10 minutes or whatever and I have to go to an update. And I said, 'Todd, I still have lots of questions to ask you. Would you be so kind as to hang around for a couple minutes?' And my program director said you can ask him to stay through the break. If they say no, you just have to accept it. Ask him ahead of time if you can. We just got Todd up just in time so I didn't have time to ask him ahead of time. And he said, 'Yeah, I'll hang around.' So it was great! Go to break, come back and I do 15 more minutes with him.

"And I said, 'Todd, I can't be thankful enough. So great. Appreciate the time.' At the time, though, I'm worried when I go to the phones that nobody's going to call, so I wanted to keep him on for a full half hour, which I did, but I didn't want to push it too, too much. So, as I'm wrapping up with him, Christensen says to me, 'What, I don't get to talk to the people of New York?' I said, 'What do you mean?' He said. 'What about the fans?' I said, 'You want to take calls with us, Todd?' and he said, 'Yeah, sure, I'll take some calls.'

"'All right, 718-937-6666 is the number. Let's talk some NFL with Todd Christensen.' So, I open up the phones. We had eight telephone lines at the time. All eight immediately light up and I'm shocked! I thought I would be talking to myself for six straight hours, no one would be calling in to this crazy show. But all eight lines are lit! I was very pleased.

"Turns out, six of the eight want to talk to me about Darryl Strawberry and the Mets, and another is a Yankees call! All that with a star guest, and only one guy wants to talk to Todd Christensen? We take the one call, we have fun with it, we clear the rest of the calls, I look up again, and the screen in front of me says they all want to talk about the Mets…again.

"So, I let Todd go, I clear those calls, and boom, they're all lit again. Turns out, I took phone calls on the Mets and Darryl Strawberry all night long! And I said, 'You know, I might be able to do this if these lines light up like this every single night.'"

A five-time Pro Bowl tight end, a guy who won two Super Bowls in a sterling career, wanted to talk some national sports with the city of New York. Not a bad, little deal, huh? There was the callers' big chance. Chat with a star, find out what it's like to suit up and take the field as a Raider each and every week. Speak with greatness. Connect with the Silver & Black.

And the callers just weren't all that interested. They wanted to talk Mets. They wanted to talk Darryl, "The Straw That Stirs the Drink." They wanted to talk with the man known as Jody Mac.

And along the way, albeit ever so slowly, an identity, a culture was being cultivated in that decrepit basement at 34-12 36th Street in Astoria. WFAN was about the city, about the sports teams in and around the city, and, more importantly, about the sports fans who helped make up the fabric of the city.

Nothing else mattered.

"That's New York for you," McDonald said.

2

Imus in the Morning on The Fan

You had to be prepared for anything. That's just the way it was with him. [Don] Imus was one of those guys who, quite frankly, wanted you to come on and have fun. It really went however you wanted to take it. If you allowed yourself to be bullied, then you were bullied. If you bit back, if he insulted you and you insulted him back, we had fun doing it. It was a one-of-a-kind show, Imus with all his sidekicks. It was a good time. It was a game changer.

—RUSS SALZBERG

JEFF SMULYAN, A PASSIONATE, PERSEVERANT CEO who prided himself on making the right moves at the right time, and his crew at Emmis Communications were at a crossroads in 1988.

WFAN was losing money. A lot of it. The talent was coming and going, a revolving door of varied hosts who struggled because they weren't a fit for New York, or New York wasn't a fit for them.

Smulyan still believed in the concept, of course, and there were times where he'd get chills listening to an old play-by-play clip, or hearing a caller who just connected the right way with the on-air talent at the time. Didn't matter the subject. Didn't matter the slot. Keith Hernandez's fielding percentage as a midday topic. Phil Simms' receiving corps as a nighttime theme. He knew there was *still* something there. He knew there were times when both sides of the phone line *just got it.*

But they didn't get it enough.

"Probably six months into the project, we did research and it showed 85 percent of all sports fans listened to WINS [1010] and WCBS [880] for scores and sports information, and not WFAN," Smulyan said.

And while he truly felt in his heart of hearts that all-sports radio and New York could still be a healthy marriage, he had to admit that less than a year into the union, divorce was a possibility.

"Change is a part of this business," he said succinctly. "So we thought about some changes."

In the end, though, the push forward was a better concept to Smulyan than was retreat. He wanted this. You can still hear that determination, that stick-to-it-iveness in his voice, more than a quarter century later. He was going to make this work. He knew it could. So, Emmis journeyed on, and became stronger along the way.

Just because WFAN was losing money didn't mean that Emmis didn't have any left. Keep in mind, this was an empire Smulyan was building, a behemoth in the world of radio that wasn't going to cling itself to just one concept, one station, one hope.

Emmis used its resources to breathe new life into WFAN. And it started with a much-needed change of the dial.

Quite simply, 1050 AM wasn't strong enough to carry Smulyan's dreams on its not-so-broad shoulders. Around certain pockets of the five boroughs, there was plenty of static to go with your Yankees and Mets scores because of the weak signal. Over in parts of New Jersey, you couldn't get it at all.

In response, Smulyan, in his next wave of purchases, bought five stations from NBC, highlighted by one with a terrific signal. WNBC was the proud tenant of 660 AM, a giant of a signal that was easily picked up in all corners of the New York metropolitan area and beyond. On a clear day, you could tune in 660 well into New England, as well as to parts of Pennsylvania and Ohio.

And after dark? On a clear night, the signal reached certain portions of north and central Florida, where many New York retirees could tune in and hear just a little taste of the old country.

"It's a monster," said Mike Lindsley, who grew up a sports radio junkie in Syracuse, New York, some 265 miles from Queens. But the distance meant little to his dreams, as he often tuned into WFAN, determinedly on his way to becoming the midday host at The Score 1260 AM in his hometown. He now has a show on 104.5 FM, The Team, an ESPN affiliate in Albany, New York. "To pick it up in Syracuse? Oh yeah, not a problem. I wouldn't be surprised to see them figure out how to someday pick up that signal in Europe."

That "monster" of a signal was Smulyan's ticket. Let's not call it a get-out-of-jail-free card, since the purchase of those five stations cost around $120 million, but 660 was a way to further deliver upon this dream. And the acquisition of 660 was about more than just the signal.

"There was a lot that went with the purchase," he said. "When we purchased the station, we inherited the talent that was under contract with the station."

The most important piece of that talent was one Don Imus, the quintessential morning radio host who could change a station's direction almost instantaneously. He was the ultimate shock jock at the time, and would take on all comers from all walks of life. A true, dyed-in-the-wool sports nut he was not. But at the time, it didn't matter. Imus was marketable. Imus was controversial. Imus was loud.

Imus was not Greg Gumbel.

"We always knew that we needed broader appeal in the morning. Even at an all-sports radio station, we had to branch out," Smulyan said. "That was our original idea for the concept. We knew we needed *Imus in the Morning*. He was under contract at NBC, and we inherited the contract.

"Today, people listen to *Mike and Mike* [on syndicated ESPN Radio] and some of the other morning shows, and it's like, 'Of course, sports will work in the mornings.' Maybe now, but in those days, the idea, to us, was, 'People talk about sports all day. In the morning, they already know the score of last night's game and they really don't want to do it.'

"We thought we needed a broader show. We thought Imus would be ideal because Imus appealed to the exact target [demographic]. Imus had a gigantic following among 25-to-54-year-old males in New York."

The game changer had arrived.

"With Don in the morning," said Mike Francesa, who would soon become an afternoon cohost at the station, "they had the hit they needed."

And so on Friday, October 7, 1988, a few hours before the Mets were scheduled to play the Los Angeles Dodgers in the National League Championship Series at Shea Stadium, WFAN moved from 1050 to 660 with Imus on the air from the parking lot. And in the wee morning hours of October 10, a catchy radio jingle—"Imus in the Morning on The Fan. Sports Radio 66. W-F-A-N!"—let all of New York know that Smulyan, Emmis, WFAN, and this all-sports, erector-set dream of a concept was here to stay.

"It was pretty simple, really," Imus said in his deep monotone. "They were on 1050 at the time, a position that you couldn't fucking hear if you were parked next to the transmitter. So, we were on

660, on WNBC, and that was sold to Emmis Broadcasting. So they switched FAN to 660 because quite frankly, FAN wasn't going to make it. It just wasn't.

"If that had not happened, there wouldn't be any WFAN. So, it had a lot to do with that signal, yes, and it had a lot to do with us, because we brought over the *Imus in the Morning* program, and whatever that meant. That combination was the difference.

"They didn't have anyone on the station that was any good at the time. They were all awful. All of their various talk show hosts were awful. And they actually *still are*. But one thing led to another."

Indeed it did. With the help of a new face, a new show, and a new morning, WFAN had new life.

"Imus was huge. To me, anyway. I think if you had to pick seminal events for the station when they did move over to 660, Imus became the morning show, and the place would never be the same," said Ed Coleman, an original at WFAN, who is now the Mets beat reporter for the station. "He was obviously—I wouldn't say he was at the height of his popularity at that point in time—but he was well established, he was well known in the market, he had good ratings, and he was just what we needed.

"He took the tack—like he always does—that he insulted everyone around him. He insulted us on the air, which I think the listeners probably got a kick out of. And I think it made people stick around."

The station also benefited from the train-wreck theory in the early days of Imus at WFAN. You know, the impression that passersby—in this instance, morning listeners—will stop and stay at the scene of an accident just to see what happened, and what might happen next.

Imus, at the time a 48-year-old with plenty of career still in front of him, was in the middle of a battle with substance abuse when he moved to The Fan. In 1987, he began treatment for alcohol and cocaine abuse, so you never knew what you were going to get from one morning to the next.

Once again, this project, which was based on a huge risk to begin with, was taking yet another. But that's Smulyan for you.

"The station really languished for a year, and Emmis is a place where everybody needles everybody, and this was sort of known as my folly. I took it in stride," Smulyan said. "Jim Lampley called it 'the Vietnam War of Emmis.' It was kind of tough. It was a tough time. And Jim wasn't alone. When we bought NBC a year later, the bankers asked me, 'How long are you going to stick with this stupid idea?'

"And we said, 'Well, we're going to transition it to 660 which is a better signal, and we're going to see what Imus can do.' People forget of course that at the time we were inheriting a Don Imus who just came out of rehab."

Whatever it took, Smulyan was willing to try it. He was going to journey onward with this thing. No matter what his new morning man might be going through, Smulyan was unfazed.

"Then there was Mike Lynn, Don's agent. Mike was a friend because he represented [former Los Angeles–area morning radio host] Robert W. Morgan, who worked for us earlier [at Emmis]. We kind of laughed and said, 'Look, Don's career may be over, and this radio station may be over,' and the joke was that we also had the Mets, who had drug problems, and Imus, who had drug problems. Other than that, we were in great shape.

"So, we said, 'Let's put them all together and see what happens.' We had seen glimmers right at that time. So, we tried it…and it worked. We did some more research. That first set I talked about showed 85 percent of all sports fans still listened elsewhere. Well, a year after that, it had flipped. It was like we had 85 percent of the sports fans listening to us."

The numbers proved Smulyan was right all along: sports fans—even in New York, where they are as die-hard as they come—still want a little balance in their mornings. Maybe they work on Wall Street, and want the business news. Maybe they have a lengthy commute via the Hudson River crossings, and really want in-depth weather and traffic. Maybe, quite frankly, they are on the verge of another long day, and just wanted to laugh about something.

Imus provided all of that.

"It really was a good mix of everything, and it worked for him," Coleman said. "He did some sports in the morning, yes. He'd bring in different guys. I know when Mike Francesa first started working there, he'd bring him on every now and then, have some fun with him. He'd occasionally have [Mad] Dog [Chris Russo, Francesa's eventual partner] on, as well. It was good to break it up. More people to laugh at and laugh with.

"Dave Sims [Coleman's eventual midday show partner] and I followed him [on the air] for a number of years, and he'd make fun of us on a regular basis. Any publicity is good publicity, I suppose, and I began to find out over time that if Imus ignored you, he didn't like you. If he ripped you to death and talked about you, he liked you. That is the way he is. That's his personality. Once you got used to that, it was kind of fun."

"We didn't change anything," said Imus, when asked how much he adapted his show to fit The Fan's format. "Whatever they wanted to do, they had to make it work with us. But we had update people—people like John Minko—who were great, and [former program director] Eric Spitz was great to work with, and Mark Mason was the program director there. They all knew what they wanted as a station, and what we did as a show, and that it had to work together.

"But there was nothing that we did, or wanted to do, to make it consistent with what they were doing. Not at all. We were doing

Imus in the Morning, and they were taking sports phone calls from morons. I mean, come on!"

Intimidating as he may have been, once people realized how the Imus Game was played, most of the talent played right along. Russ Salzberg was one of them. A television sports anchor at WWOR Channel 9 in New York, Salzberg was another midday host in WFAN lore, and he took advantage of his at-bats on *Imus in the Morning*. Salzberg, who partnered with Steve Somers for a brief run on the 10:00 AM–to–1:00 PM slot, knew that being on *Imus*—in any capacity—could only help his personal profile.

"You get on *Imus*, and it promoted you," he said. "That was always something to remember. And as far as what happened when you were on there, well, it's like anything else. If you can take it, they like it, because you're bringing something to the table. You're making their show better. If you're a doormat, then you're just a doormat. After a while, that's not fun, and you won't be back a whole lot more."

But if you could hang with the man who donned a cowboy hat and a straight smile, if you could snag a seat at his table—and more importantly, keep that seat through the meal—you were set. Especially in the sports-update slot. After all, if you were on *Imus in the Morning* to give a sports update, you had to (1) deliver the goods to a hard-core sports audience who needed all the information in a short period of time, and (2) do so all while getting verbally jabbed, left and right, by the king of morning radio.

Not easy, folks.

But the list of students who passed through those doors is a long one. From personalities who moved on to carve out their own careers at WFAN—such as Francesa and Russo—to those who have excelled at new outlets—including Steve Levy [ESPN], Mike Breen [MSG Network, NBA on ESPN], and Chris Carlin [SportsNet New

York]—the *Imus* update slot is clearly one of the biggest stepping stones in all of sports broadcasting.

"There have been a lot of guys who passed through who got it. There were others who didn't," Imus said. "But it comes down to talent. The only thing that we ever talked about with updates was whether or not they had any talent to do it."

Sid Rosenberg was one of the guys who had it.

Undeniably one of the most explosive, enigmatic, yet incredibly talented personalities to ever grace the airwaves at WFAN, Rosenberg made a name for himself barreling through sports updates on the *Imus* show. He made them stand out, made them unforgettable, and in doing so, he brought the whole concept of morning sports updates to a new level.

There was news, there was comedy, there were all of the Imus-esque particulars that were needed with Rosenberg's updates, make no mistake. But he was such a fit on the Imus crew—he was equally controversial and unafraid to tempt fate, almost to a fault—that he was able to stick around a bit longer in front of the microphone than the other guys. Maybe it was style, his hard-core Brooklyn accent, his delivery. Maybe it was just the fact that he didn't walk a fine line, he walked right over it.

Whatever it was, Rosenberg had *it*. And Imus knew it.

"I was lucky. I was the only one—and I say to this day that all those guys were great, all of them—who got to stay on the show, the whole show," Rosenberg said. "I really believe Breen—in terms of the sports—was the most creative and the funniest. I love Mike Breen, but I ended up revolutionizing that role in that Breen and everybody else was there for a 10-minute sports update. I became the only guy that was in the studio four hours a day!

"Imus enjoyed it so much that he came in one day and said, 'I want Sid in the studio all day, every show.' It didn't matter if he was talking sports or if he was talking to [late journalist and lawyer] Tim Russert or whether he was talking with the president or his brother, eventually it got to the point where I was involved in almost every conversation!

"So for what it's worth—and I'm not taking credit for it—it was more Imus and the trust he had in me. I really revolutionized that position, even after I left."

The thing about Rosenberg with Imus was that they were very much alike in some way, yet opposite in others. Unequivocally intelligent yet incredibly disputatious, one talked sports—and plenty of other stuff, too, but he was there for the sports—at a thousand miles per hour. The other ran the show, and was slower with the delivery, but just as powerful and much more diverse in his targets. They fed off each other, though, and in a chair where many an update man was devoured by the top dog and his minions, Rosenberg, warts and all, had staying power.

"Again, some of that was Imus showing a lot of faith in me and thinking I could handle all of that, when it came to talking news or politics or stirring the pot," said Rosenberg, who like Imus has battled chemical addiction at various points in his career, perhaps with even more notoriety than Imus. After several struggles, Rosenberg cleaned up his image once and for all in 2012, and returned to the airwaves as his own morning host at WMEN 640 AM in South Florida.

"One of the things I pride myself on—even during my daily talk show here in Miami to this day—is that I'm a pretty well-rounded guy. It's not just about sports with me. Sometimes I got myself into trouble up there because I had a tendency to want to talk more about news stuff, or political stuff, or entertainment stuff, and I had to be constantly reminded, 'You're on a sports talk station, okay? I know you're getting bored talking about [former New York Mets shortstop] Kaz Matsui's batting average. I know you don't want to talk about another bad [former New York Giants quarterback] Kerry Collins interception, but that's what you're here to do.'

"Even to this day, it still happens. I get called into the principal's office and he says, 'You're great, we love you, you're a great listen, but don't forget what you're here for, you know?' On *Imus*, he allowed me to do all that. It was a perfect mix. I was saying things that Imus wanted to say.

"Early in his career, he would say that kind of stuff, but he got to the point with all of his controversies that he had to slow it down. He started doing all this great charitable work and talking with the presidents, senators, and congressmen, and he just couldn't do some of that stuff anymore. It didn't make sense that Don Imus would talk to the president and then say something as outlandish as the things I would say. But he was thinking it, you know? And the listener was thinking it.

"So, I became that mouthpiece, and I was all too willing to do it. I just wanted to make him happy and get my name out there. And it worked at times. It was great. It was genius for all of us."

But Imus was the marquee mouthpiece long before Rosenberg joined the crew in 2001. Many a headline was garnered by Imus, both good and bad, across parts of three decades at WFAN.

More importantly, with all those headlines came ratings, advertising dollars, and plenty of notoriety. Indeed, The Fan soon became Imus' land. Whether it was a memorable parody of Imus interviewing any number of religious cardinals, in the form of Bernard McGuirk, his executive producer; or one of his several personality-shaping, industry-rattling interviews with Bill Clinton (before and after he was elected president); or one of his unabashed rip jobs on fellow WFAN employees—think "Fatso and Froot Loops," instead of "Mike and the Mad Dog," the eventual name of the Francesa and Russo afternoon show that further laid the foundation for the station—nothing was out of bounds for the I-Man. Nothing.

Which suited the folks at The Fan just fine.

"Well, Imus was certainly the turning point. I think the brilliance of Imus within that format is often overlooked," said Howie Rose, an original host in Astoria, whose incredible feel for the radio business has converged ever so eloquently with his New York upbringing and encyclopedic sports mind across the life of this station. Few people have fit more seamlessly into the WFAN household than Rose, and even fewer have anywhere near his razor-sharp memory of nearly every step this station has taken since Smulyan's dream became a reality.

"I don't get the sense that everyone really understands the true genius of Imus as he related to WFAN. Looking back, he could have very easily gone into the studio, sat down, and said, 'Hey, I'm Imus in the morning. I've been doing this in New York since the early 1970s. I'm not changing anything about my show. You're picking it up because you need a morning show. And sports—in and of itself—is just not going to work in the morning. So, I'm here. This is my show and all I'm going to be is what I've been since 1971 in New York.'

"What he did so brilliantly was begin to incorporate sports genuinely. He likes sports even though he can make you think otherwise, but the brilliance of Imus in those early days is that he began to incorporate sports into his show and created this sort of symbiotic relationship...even though he would joke about who's listening after his show was over, and make fun of all of us who were trying to make sports radio work."

Indeed, he'd try to play dumb around the jocks, so to speak. And it was great radio and terrific theater.

Simple, at times, yes. But superb most of the time. And polarizing all the time.

"Who'd the Knicks play last night again?"

"Philadelphia, Don."

"Are they the 76ers?"

"Yes."

"Right. Okay. Carry on."

Even if he knew the answers—which he did more often than not—he pretended that he didn't to allow his sports-update men to deliver some news, some wit, some charm, and then kick it back to the I-Man before they got ripped again. He was giving them a stage on which to perform.

That stage was available to more than up-and-coming professionals eager to strut their stuff on his show. Imus and the WFAN management team would often branch out and take a chance on a long shot. And there was no bigger long shot on *Imus in the Morning* than Evan Roberts. For starters, well, he wasn't even shaving yet.

"I'm young enough where I grew up with the radio station. I don't know a world without WFAN because it came around when I was four years old," said Roberts, a quintessential New York sports fan, but also a longtime student of radio who is now a midday host at WFAN. "From the moment I was six and on, I was listening to the station all the time, and I would imitate it in my bedroom when I was seven, eight, nine years old. I would literally have my own WFAN. It wasn't great imitation. I tried to do Chris Russo and Mike Francesa, but they weren't great imitations. I just wanted to be a talk show host.

"I wrote a letter to, I think it was [sales manager] Joel Hollander at the time and [operations manager] Mark Chernoff, basically applying for a job. I remember I made a tape on my little tape recorder and sent it to them saying, 'Hire me!' I don't know what the hell I was thinking. I was nine years old!

"And the memory I have is my mom and dad coming into my bedroom, saying, 'We got a message you need to hear.' I was like okay. And they let me listen to a message from Chernoff, who's now my boss, saying, 'Hey, we heard your tape. We'd love to have you in with Imus.' I was freaking out! I was like, wow, this is fantastic! I never really listened to Imus. I'm nine years old. I like sports. I knew Imus, but I wasn't listening to his show all that often, no offense to him. That's how I remember getting the opportunity to go on Imus. I don't remember anything specific of the experience other than walking through the dungeon of WFAN and getting there. I remember my mom and dad were with me, and I was handwriting the updates. When you're nine, it's so tough to have vivid memories. I don't remember anything about being on."

All that said, he'll never forget a quick conversation he had with the I-Man, one of those rare behind-the-scenes moments that help to make Imus…Imus.

"I just remember being nervous and talking to Imus after the broadcast, and he was giving me advice on getting into the business," Roberts said. "And while I grew up and did other radio jobs, I always kind of knew my goal was eventually to get back to The Fan. It took a couple years, but I got back there."

In addition to adding fuel to the fire that already burned in people like Roberts, Imus and the WFAN management team were also gaining new listeners. Imus was pulling in fans who had followed him every step of his career—some of whom had little interest in sports—and he was getting them to stick around after his show to listen to "all sports, all the time."

This way, The Fan could hit the ratings game from several angles. As Rose said, "true genius."

"I think that first year until Imus came aboard," he said, "I used to come in every day and look over my shoulder to see if that was the day they were going to padlock the doors. I just never knew. None of us did.

"Then he came along and absolutely changed everything."

In doing so, Imus set a new standard for hosts at the fledgling station. Whether you were talking news, politics, weather, and sports—like Imus—or you were talking just sports—like everyone else at The Fan—you had to play up to his level, or else the station wasn't going to be consistent and achieve that level of reliability required of any 24-hours-a-day, seven-days-a-week outfit.

And playing up to his level? Well, Imus was a tough act to follow.

It didn't take long for Jody McDonald to learn that the hard way. A true sportsaholic who extracts the absolute best out of his callers, McDonald had that unenviable task quite often. Among several time slots McDonald has worked during his off-and-on tenure at The Fan was the 10:00 AM–to–1:00 PM midday spot. Imus would exit. McDonald—most of the time with one of several partners, including Rosenberg—would enter.

Not that there's any pressure or anything, Jody. It's only Imus we're talking about, right?

"Yeah, something like that. Well, we knew a couple of things going in. We knew we had to have a different audience at 10:00 AM, because the people listening to Imus weren't necessarily tuning in for us. And the people tuning in for us weren't necessarily tuned into Imus at 6:30 AM," McDonald said. "Imus was the reason the radio station became what it was. There's absolutely no question. He brought an audience that the station didn't have before, credibility and the like. If there wasn't a Don Imus, I don't know if there ever would have been a WFAN and the sports explosion that it became.

"But, all that said, it still didn't make it any easier for the show that came after him, which was a straight sports show, when Imus' wasn't. Although he tried. He had Breen in there, and he had Sid in there. He didn't turn his nose up at sports. He tried to at least dabble in it so there was some connection to the rest of the station.

"But I think that was a hill the midday people had to climb the whole time Imus was there."

And it wasn't any easier for Imus' table setters, either. The overnight hosts kept the seat warm for Imus and took sports calls from drunks and vagabonds until 5:30 AM. They had to deal with the loneliness of the graveyard shift, the anonymity of being on, quite frankly, when most everyone else was off. There they were—far too many of them to name over the years—working in a ghost town of a studio while everyone else was at home, tucked away neatly in their beds with care. By the time Team Imus showed up to begin preparing for the morning show, well, at least the overnight guys had someone to talk to during the breaks.

But that wasn't always the case. Imus, especially as the years passed by, would pick and choose who he'd talk to. And sometimes he just wasn't in the mood to chat.

"That's the thing with me. Strange, but the thing about Imus was, I never met the guy. Never met him," said Kevin Burkhardt, sort of a forgotten yet successful and smooth overnight host who blew through The Fan in the early 2000s on his way to becoming the television field reporter for the Mets on SportsNet New York. "There were plenty of times I did overnights leading into his show, and you'd think we'd pass by in the night. Well, never once met him. Don't know him from Adam.

"He was kind of a ghost when I was there. Even the times in the morning when I would come in and he was doing his show, he kind of seemed like an unapproachable guy. I never really had the urge to make that happen."

Imus could certainly be that way. As a result, many less experienced staff members tiptoed around the newsroom when in his presence, hesitant to say or do the wrong thing.

Just ask Levy, a proud, passionate New Yorker with big dreams who would later graduate to ESPN and call quite a few hockey games there. He eventually landed in the top anchor spot for the network's signature program, *SportsCenter*, and still appears there quite regularly.

But back in the day, Levy was at The Fan, feeling his way through the business. One day, not long after he made it to the station, he got the call to be Imus' sports-update man. He had been doing updates on other shows, and some odds and ends around the station, but this was it. This was *the* gig.

Imus' update guy? The chance of a lifetime? Where did you want Levy to sign?

"So, yeah, I did *Imus* for three weeks before Mike Breen took over. Breen became a star off of the Imus stuff. I tried, but I was way too young for the job. It was morning drive. It was Imus. It was his time of day. His stage, not mine. And quite frankly, I wasn't funny. I'm still not funny to this day," Levy said, ever so humbly.

Don't believe him, by the way. Levy always was able to mix in just the right bit of humor on his NHL telecasts for ESPN, and wouldn't be sitting in the big chair on Sunday nights during *SportsCenter* if he didn't have some sort of "funny" in him. More proof? Levy, who has made the absolute most of the stage that ESPN provides for its stars, has appeared in several movies through the years; all six—*Parental Guidance* (2012), *Tooth Fairy* (2010), *The Game Plan* (2007), *The Ringer* (2005), *Fever Pitch* (2005), and *Mystery, Alaska* (1999)—are listed, not surprisingly, as comedies.

"I was nervous. I was intimidated," Levy said. "All the guys were on me. [News-update man] Chuck [McCord], all the guys behind the scenes, Bernie [McGuirk], you name it, all those guys. I could do no right.

"Don wasn't particularly nice, either, but he kept me on for three weeks. The story I will tell you—and I've never told this in public—is that I got called into Mark Mason's office one day and he said, 'Look, this is not working out.' I was disappointed, but I felt it was coming. I was in over my head. I was not funny. And I needed to be funny. And that just wasn't what I was all about.

"Mark tells me that the project is over, and I was a little disappointed that they chose to put somebody else on the show. I won't lie. But I get back to my computer the next day, and the computers there had these top-line messages on them. Way at the top, you could instant message someone. It was like a retro form of texting.

"Well, in parentheses would be the name of who the message was from. So, I get there, log on, and in parenthesis, it said 'Imus,' and I'm like 'Great. What now?' But I look, and the message says, 'Hey, you don't suck.' That was the exact quote."

Only Imus can give a vote of confidence, a pat on the back, and ignite a tremendous career in broadcasting by using the word *suck* in a one-line message.

"That's what it said, and to me that was a human side of Don that people just don't see," Levy said. "That made me feel really good. He respected me enough to do that. If he didn't care, he wouldn't have said anything. That was a little side, I thought, that no one knows.

"Unless someone wrote it for him from his computer, I've always taken that as a positive from Don Imus. To this day, that's the only job I wanted that I never really succeeded at. It was a case of being rushed to the majors too soon. I was not professionally prepared to be in that sports spot, and Mike Breen took it and ran with it. Mike was great at it and has gone on to bigger and better things, for sure. I graduated from college in 1987, so I might have been just a little too young. This was a time when they were rotating guys in and out of sports for Imus, trying to find the right mix. They were trying to find him a main sports guy. I wasn't it.

"I gave it a shot. I lasted more than a lot of people did. So many others were chewed up and spit out. I lasted three weeks. I took that for what it was worth, but I'll never forget how it ended and what Imus wrote to me. It really meant a lot."

In many ways, Levy's experience is a microcosm of Imus' overall effect at The Fan. In the course of less than a month, Levy went from being intimidated by Imus to being inspired by him. No longer did he fear Imus. Now, he was fueled by Imus.

And through the ups and the downs, in good times and in bad, might the same be said for Don and WFAN, all told? In his unique way, he influenced and motivated *everyone* at The Fan to be better than they were the day before.

"Well, he's one of a kind. I don't think there's any question about that," Coleman said of the I-Man. "For several reasons, it just worked for him here at The Fan...for a long, long time."

3

Good Afternoon, Everybody! How Are You Today?

I remember [Don] Imus said to me once, "You have to listen to [Chris] Russo. He sounds like Donald Duck on steroids. But really listen to him, because he is very entertaining." And he was right, of course. Mike Francesa, well, he was a guy, I think, who tried to get any job at FAN because he loved the idea. He was working as a producer at CBS and I think he had to beg everybody to get an on-air shift on the weekends. And it was clear he had an encyclopedic knowledge of sports— he was always sort of the brains of the operation. And I think the idea was, let's try these guys together, see what happens. One guy knows sports better than anybody and the other guy is entertaining. It was fortuitous. Sometimes you do that in radio...and it just works.

—JEFF SMULYAN

MANY MISTAKES WERE MADE during the early years of WFAN. That's understandable, of course; all stations make them, and The

Fan, perhaps above all others, has made more than enough right decisions to overwhelm the wrong ones.

"Oh, but there were some *wrong* ones," John Minko, a longtime update man and an original staffer at WFAN, said. "Those early days? Yeah, lotta mistakes."

Pete Franklin was one of them.

Franklin developed a sports brand—and a name for himself—at WWWE AM 1100 in Cleveland. He had a rough exterior and a rougher way with his callers, but with the help of some props and sound effects, he managed to entertain the Ohio masses daily. And he didn't need winning teams to keep him going, either, like so many sports talk show hosts do. No, he got by just fine by knocking those woebegone Browns and the hapless Indians all afternoon long...and listeners loved him for it.

Jeff Smulyan noticed, and he felt Franklin would fit right in to what he was building at WFAN. Smulyan, of course, wasn't confusing Frank Sinatra's "New York, New York" for "Cleveland, Cleveland," but he saw something in the Ohio radio veteran. Even in the media capital of the world, he felt Franklin could stir up some callers. He felt he'd spark debate. And, if the ratings went along with him and some advertisers opened up their wallets, well, all the better.

But it wasn't meant to be. First, Franklin suffered a heart attack before leaving Cleveland. So as Smulyan launched this courageous WFAN ship from its port, it was without its afternoon, drive-time host. It was without *their* guy.

So, fill-ins—a dime a dozen—took their swings, and fanned a lot, as Franklin recovered and prepared for New York. Eventually, he made it there. But he left his success back in northeast Ohio.

"There's no question we brought in Pete Franklin from Cleveland to be *the* star of the lineup," Smulyan said. "Pete was really the king of Cleveland and we brought him into New York. He *wasn't* the king of New York."

The ratings proved it. Even in the Big Apple, he was a little too gruff for the fans and often insulted the callers, who were obviously the lifeblood of the station. Eventually, people stopped listening. People stopped calling. And before too long, even Franklin caught on to it.

Franklin, who died November 23, 2004, resigned from his post two months before his two-year contract ran its course at WFAN, and suddenly, Smulyan had a gaping afternoon hole to fill.

"It was a labor of love," he said. "It was an important show to find, but we were eager to find something that worked, something that fit."

They found it.

Chris Russo was an energetic, ear-splitting bolt of energy with an unforgettable voice who was young, hungry, and ready to make a name for himself. He couldn't pronounce names all that well, but the New York native was simply ecstatic just to be in that monster of a market. Everything else, well, he could work on.

Russo had done updates on *Imus in the Morning* after toiling around the business in Florida, making pit stops in places such as Orlando and Jacksonville. Odd jobs aplenty. He eventually made his way to New York, built up an image, and drew some interest from Smulyan.

"I was fortunate. No question, fortunate. Right place, right time," said Russo, as he delivered his patented, quick-hitting—and sometimes repetitive—sentences to prove his point. "I always loved sports and I always wanted to be a play-by-play guy. I thought that's where I was going to go, more for the play-by-play standpoint than anything else. Marv Albert I always loved as a kid. I listened to [New York Yankees radio play-by-play announcer John] Sterling do sports talk and the NCAA tournament as a kid, and I loved it. I thought more play-by-play than anything else. That's what I was going to do.

"I ended up at Rollins College in Winter Park, Florida, and they had a radio station. I deejayed, I did some play-by-play. Still didn't think I'd get involved in the talk-radio format. But it's funny how things happen. After going to the winter meetings for baseball, I applied for a play-by-play job—making a brief stop in Jacksonville trying to get a play-by-play job with the Jacksonville Suns [a minor league baseball team]. So, I ended up there, in a local radio station in Jacksonville doing sports talk, and I sort of fell into it. I realized I had a knack for it. I worked in Jacksonville for a year. I got a show—it was a dawn-to-dusk station, so I worked there from May to March. I was fortunate. It was daylight savings time and it went off the air at 9:00 PM in the summertime. So I was able to stay on the air two, three hours a day. Late in the afternoon, 5:00 until 8:00, or 4:30 to 7:00, that kind of thing. And I did sports talk. This is in '83, '84. I learned I could do it. And I loved it.

"And then I ended up in Orlando shortly thereafter because I had a friend of mine who was a Rollins graduate, who was a producer of a talk show down at WKIS [AM 740]. I ended up in Orlando and was there for three years. Again, right place, right time—that means a lot in this business. Don't let anyone tell you otherwise. This is early '84, I was there for about three, three and a half years.

"So, my apprenticeship was in a small town from a radio perspective, but big cities overall. Orlando and Jacksonville are decent-sized cities. It's not like I was in Racine, Wisconsin. I was in a decent-sized town and that ended up helping me get to New York. I found my niche—which is the most important thing—and then I ended up at WMCA [AM 570] in '88. And before you know it, I was at FAN with Don Imus. It all moved quickly."

Mike Francesa, also a New Yorker, had far less mileage on his resume. Equipped with an accent to prove it, he graduated from St. John's in Jamaica, Queens, and was built to succeed in sports media in his home city. There was no exile in Florida for Francesa. He took on a job in television at CBS, and kept all other avenues open. But it was always about New York for him, nowhere else.

"I heard about WFAN during the '86 [Major League Baseball] playoffs, that they were starting an all-sports station. I didn't know exactly what that would entail. When I found out, I inquired about a position. They thought I was applying to be a producer. I wasn't. I was applying to be a show host," Francesa said, delivering a history lesson not unlike the way he delivers a show opening—detailed and driven. "They said they were bringing in national show hosts from around the country. None of those positions were going to be open. From a production standpoint, they thought with my television background, I was overqualified. I said I was looking for on-air. They said that wasn't the way they were going. So, basically it went nowhere."

But connections hold a lot of value in this business, and Francesa had them. He still does. He also had a determination to get in there and stay there. He still does.

"A friend of mine knew one of the guys who was running the place. Said to him he thought I would be a good guy to take a shot on for a show. They eventually said yes and they let me cohost on the weekend, doing some football shows. That's how it kind of started," Francesa said. "I got my foot in the door, and from there I went to fill in for a lot of the hosts, especially Pete Franklin, who was sick. I filled in for Pete over Thanksgiving and then after that they used me a lot as a fill-in host for a lot of their hosts—for Jim Lampley or for Spencer Ross, guys who were missing shows."

Along the way, he was stockpiling experience and constructing an image at the station. Slowly but surely, he was becoming what people said he wouldn't be: a full-time talk show host at WFAN.

"After that—people forget this one little interlude—but they decided that WFAN was going to be the WINS of sports," he said. WINS AM 1010 is the country's first all-news station that is famous for its nickname—"Ten-Ten Wins"—as well as its slogan—"All news, all the time. You give us 22 minutes, we'll give you the world."

"The station was doing really badly, and they decided they were going to make it a WINS of sports," Francesa said. "They were going to go away from having hosts with opinions and personalities to just do an every-20-minute revolving update and really make it magazine-type, really quick-hitting, very timed sports. All the time.

"And they weren't looking for show hosts, suddenly. So, that kind of stopped everybody in their tracks. But that didn't last long. That idea went by the boards within about a month. Then they were back to looking for show hosts again."

Just like that, he was back in the game and closer than ever to the promised land.

"Then the program director, who would have been the third program director, Mark Mason, took a liking to me and started putting me on more. He put me on a lot in the summer. I took advantage. Then I started getting put in the midday and I went in and did a couple shows in the afternoon, and it was really good," he said.

"After that came the idea of *Mike and the Mad Dog*. And that was that."

Indeed it was. As Smulyan watched from afar, he noticed the two guys attacking the microphone in different ways with similar results. They knew sports, they knew New York, and they both had enough confidence in themselves to succeed at The Fan.

Smulyan didn't share that surplus of confidence at first, but he knew he was onto something. He had a hunch that *Mike and the Mad Dog* could work in New York.

"I looked at it like a marriage. If you spend five hours or four hours a day with your wife, you're going to have differences. Think about that. Four hours a day with somebody, it is like a marriage," Smulyan said, laughing. "Sometimes things would be great and sometimes they wouldn't get along. But if all of that played out on the air and entertained, then it was worth it."

It was a risk, of course. In many ways, Francesa and Russo were on the opposite end of the spectrum from Franklin. They were a pair as opposed to a solo act; they were young, fresh faces, as opposed to being a nationally recognized name. But above all else, they were largely unproven, not as founts of sports knowledge who could work a room with character, color, and charisma—they could do that just fine—but as cohosts who could carry the afternoon shift in such a huge market. They had what it took to make it work—the skills, the stones, the substance, you name it—but would that play out across 25-plus hours a week? It was a tough task.

"I will never forget my absolute original thought," said Howie Rose, an original employee at WFAN who may possess more knowledge of the inner workings of the station than anyone and can easily be the station's walking encyclopedia. "I was walking with [WFAN sales manager] Joel Hollander toward the subway station from the studios. As we were crossing a corner, he tells me, 'Listen to what I think we're going to do with afternoon drive.' It was clear Pete Franklin wasn't working and they had to make a change there. And Joel said, 'What do you think of this? What do you think of putting Russo and Francesa together?' And my very, very, very, very first reaction was, 'You got to be kidding!' And 10 seconds later I thought... *It's fucking brilliant.*

"I said, 'This is so ridiculous it could work!' And I think that was probably the universal feeling among those who came up with it. My recollection is the guy who initially thought of it was Mark Mason. He had so much to do with saving that station. My initial thoughts were probably similar to many others: *Mike's going to steamroll him. Mike's not going to have any patience for Chris.* And it's going to be incumbent on Russo not only to fight for himself but to do it in a disarming way, to try making Mike sound a little less clinical than he sounded originally. And, what do you know? It worked!"

Indeed it did. On September 5, 1989, *Mike and the Mad Dog* debuted with one host, Francesa, sporting a serious, surefire attitude and translating it into everything he said, and the other, Russo, throwing caution to the wind and his hands in the air, just letting loose. They were such opposites, they attracted everyone's attention.

"This is where you can come back to the brilliance of Imus in those early days," Rose said. "What he did for Russo and Francesa—and this is a little bit later, after he came on to WFAN, obviously—is he helped make Russo and Francesa's ascent possible by creating more than just a tension. He created a curiosity about them that drove listeners to tune in later in the day."

And they did, in droves. Quickly, *Mike and the Mad Dog* took off and easily became the most important non-morning show at the station, and perhaps all of New York, for that matter. Because that's what it was at the end of the day. It was a New York sports show, through and through.

"I remember Mike and Chris, when they got together, that was a good show. A really good show," Imus said. "But the other shows were awful and they remain awful."

The one that wasn't awful in Imus' eyes almost never happened. In fact, if one of the two hosts had his way back in the 1980s, it might have been a solo show.

"Well, it was very much a shotgun marriage," Francesa said in a passionate, proud interview. "They put us together. They told me I was in the afternoon. I said, 'Great.' They then said that it was going to be with someone else, and I knew who Chris was, but I hadn't worked with him or anything. I hardly knew him.

"They said, 'We have an idea for a show: *Mike and the Mad Dog.* We want you to go home over the weekend and think about this idea of *Mike and the Mad Dog.*' I said okay, but I said, 'Can I have it by myself?' They said 'No. It's either *Mike and the Mad Dog* or it's nothing.'

"They obviously had to convince me. I tried to talk them out of it, but it was obvious what they wanted. One of the things that I didn't know that I learned later—and it shows you how naïve I was in the business—I didn't realize I was doing well in the afternoon by myself. I didn't even know enough to check the ratings to see what I was doing by myself. Well, I was moving well by myself and I didn't realize it, didn't know I could have made any demands. I wasn't in a position to, I didn't think. I wasn't even aware where the ratings were or anything, so I didn't realize I had done well when they decided to make that decision.

"I don't know if I could've used it to my advantage, anyway. I probably couldn't have. I was so naïve. They were adamant about *Mike and the Mad Dog.* I knew it was the only way to get the show that I really wanted. From the moment I walked in there, I really wanted to do afternoon drive. I really wanted to do it. I even went in one day and told them that if they gave me the opportunity, I'd be there 15 years in the afternoon drive. That was 25 years ago. They said, 'Go in with the Mad Dog or you don't go.' So, to me, it wasn't much of a choice. They told me what I was going to be paid. They offered me a three-year contract with no negotiation. They offered me a partner with no negotiation.

"I learned a lot of lessons. One of them one was, if you want to get involved in these negotiations, you have to have a little leverage. I always tried to take leverage into my deals in the future. But at that time, all I did was say, 'Yes, yes, yes, and yes.' Because I didn't have anyone or anywhere to go."

It wasn't all bad, of course. Together, Francesa and Russo were living the dream, and separately, they were getting paid well. And after wading through the tough times early on—swinging and missing with national hosts, and watching advertisers look elsewhere—WFAN had finally found a daytime elixir.

"Shotgun marriage? Mike and me? Absolutely," Russo said. "We didn't know each other that well. I knew Mike from around the station, but we came from completely different backgrounds. Mike came from the TV sports background, and I came from the radio background. I think in the end that helped us, but at the time it was a little weird because I didn't know where his background was from and he didn't know where my background was from.

"I think we realized they weren't going to give us a show by ourselves, so if we were going to do 2:00-to-7:00—and at the time I think it was 3:00-to-7:00—if they were going to give us that time slot, we were going to have to share it. End of story. I think we went into it realizing it was too good to turn down, and we were going to have to deal with a partner if we wanted that half a piece of the pie. And that was that. From that standpoint, although we probably went into it not loving the partnership idea, I think we realized—end of the day—it was too good of a situation to pass up.

"Now, it wasn't like we had practice. It wasn't like there were shows in that summer of '89 to get us used to each other. I don't remember—I'm sure we did—but I don't remember day after day of meetings. We had some issues. We did. You're putting two guys together on the radio who don't know that much about each other.

We didn't grow up together—we both grew up in New York—but different. I had only been at FAN for a short period of time. I got there in December and here I am with Mike five, six months later. Shotgun marriage."

Smulyan concurs with the assessment. After all, he was the one who arranged the marriage.

"I always say I've done some things really right and some things really wrong," Smulyan said. "We were fortunate—the people in place made the right decision, it worked, and it's something I'm very proud of."

The show followed a template from one day to the next. Russo and Francesa would address the hottest topic of the day after a top-of-the-hour sports update. Traditionally, that opening segment would last from five minutes past the hour until about 19 minutes past, and then came another update. Shortly after the update and some commercials, the two would come back, open up what Russo would always label "your two-way, sports talk telephone number," and then get to work.

"We eventually triggered some connections, some chemistry," Russo said. "Basically we went into it, two radio guys thrown together, and let's see if they can mesh. That's exactly what it was. It was up to me and Mike to make it work. We had too much to lose if we didn't and it was too good of an opportunity to screw it up. They were depending on us to get the show together. Eventually, after a lot of hit and miss, a lot of issues, we came to have an understanding of how to do this.

"It took years, but eventually we got a feel of each other a little bit, and we had some good sports stuff going on, too. The Giants won the Super Bowl [in 1991] and then, of course, a couple years later, the Rangers and Knicks do what they do [in 1994, winning the Stanley Cup and losing in the NBA Finals, respectively].

"To make a long story short, we had success, which is always nice, and we really found our way. But it wasn't like it was well-planned out in the summer before we began in September of '89. Not at all."

But isn't that what WFAN was all about? Sure, Smulyan planned and plotted. But clearly there was a lot of "let's throw it on the wall and see if it sticks" to it all. For those two guys, well, they stuck.

"Two different people, for sure, but what made it so great was Mike and Chris were just two guys talking sports," said Eric Spitz, former program director at WFAN and now the boss at the CBS Sports Radio Network. "We like to look at things in the POKE scale—passion, opinion, knowledge, and entertainment. And certainly if you look at the POKE scale—if you combine the two guys—the passion, opinion, knowledge, and entertainment, they're 10s across the board. No doubt. No question. Elevens and 12s if you can rank them that high.

"Those two guys had enough to talk about, they had different backgrounds, and it all came together. Mike was more of the New York sports fan. Obviously a huge Yankees fan. Over the years, he's been a Giants fan, a Knicks fan, a Rangers fan. Chris was a San Francisco Giants fan. Chris really didn't have a football team, and hockey and basketball I don't think he had teams there, either. If he had the chance to back a football team, I think he would have chosen the Packers years ago. Now I don't think he even would probably choose one.

"But with Mike being a New York sports fan, and Chris' unique ability to go on the radio and speak with passion about the teams that he didn't even like, was huge and I think very underrated. Chris could deliver it, not in a phony way at all. Chris could get on the Giants or Jets or Yankees or Mets and talk about them in such a passionate way, you would think he was a fan of the team. I think that resonates with the listener.

"What Mike and Chris did was just talk sports. There was no phoniness to it. It wasn't like they were on stage. It wasn't like you turned the mic on or the camera on, and they morphed into 'Mike and the Mad Dog.' You can pull it off maybe a little while that way, but that was genuine. Mike and Chris talking in the newsroom before the show, or Mike and Chris talking during the breaks during the show, or talking to you after the show—it's the same thing as *the* show. That to me was one of the main reasons why they were so successful—they were genuine. It was two guys, really passionate about sports with really strong opinions about sports with great knowledge."

A key factor in the show's success was the hosts' ability to wrap themselves around big events, not let go, and use every minute of every show to give the listeners what they wanted. Whether it was Super Bowl week—when they'd go on location and broadcast NFL-themed shows, complete with guests galore, trivia contests, and, of course, your calls—or an exciting Yankees, Knicks, or Rangers playoff run, Francesa and Russo knew what drove New York. Big-time events meant big-time interest and big-time ratings. They embraced that.

"I think they felt, as it went along, that we appealed to the New York audience," Francesa said. "And that was the way to go. But I don't think the people who were there ever foresaw the success that was around the corner. I think they hoped they would hit on something that would give them some longevity, but I don't they ever even had an inkling—even with Don in the morning—I don't think they ever had an inkling as to what was to come."

Indeed, *Mike and the Mad Dog* became the place to be. Forget the listeners and the callers for a second. The guests—be they players, managers, coaches, agents, journalists, what have you—quickly understood that if they wanted to get their message, their mission out there, they'd best do it on *Mike and the Mad Dog*.

"Whether people loved or hated Mike *or* Chris, or Mike *and* Chris together, there's one place they want to be: on that show," said Rich Ackerman, a longtime sports-update man at WFAN who Francesa and Russo traditionally referred to as "Ack." "If they want their side of the story out, if they want the public to hear what they have to say, they wanted to do it on *Mike and the Mad Dog*. That is one piece of prime real estate."

Just ask Jay Wright, basketball coach at Villanova. Wright, who coached at Hofstra on Long Island before heading to Philadelphia and the Big East Conference, became a favorite on *Mike and the Mad Dog* and is still reaping the benefits. Back then, Hofstra's teams were known as the Flying Dutchmen—the school has since changed its moniker to the more succinct Pride—but call them what you will, Francesa and Russo wrapped their arms around them.

It proved to be a trifecta. The two hosts were tremendous college basketball fans—especially in March, when the sports world fixates on the NCAA tournament—and Wright carries the right kind of charm, color, and cheer to carry a show himself.

"When I was at Hofstra, we were trying to make a name. When we first got there, we were 295th out of 302 Division I teams," Wright said, looking back on a frustrating but worthwhile time. "And Mike and the Mad Dog were huge for us. At the time, Hofstra was really trying to build, and we had an admissions director named Mary Beth Carey, and she used to do these commercials on WFAN: 'Hi, I'm Mary Beth Carey. Come to Hofstra.' So as a result, WFAN would have me on all the time. Mike and the Mad Dog would put me on to talk Hofstra basketball and people were like, 'What is this guy doing on the air? Hofstra is awful!' And they were right.

"But Mike and Chris never wavered on that, because we had a relationship, and it grew from there. Then, we started getting a little better, and they'd have me on, and Hofstra people were really getting into it! We hadn't done anything really as a program, but since the coach was on a show like *Mike and the Mad Dog*, it was a source of pride. Just like that, and that's because those two guys were so big. They were such big time then—this is '94, '95, '96—and they kept having us small-timers on!

"We were at Hofstra seven years. In our fourth or fifth year, one day they came to me and said, 'If you guys make the America East championship, we'll do the game live.' So, in our sixth year, we get the America East championship game at home, and it's at 11:00 in the morning. And Mike and Chris came out and did the whole game! Chris did the play-by-play; Mike did the color. It was Hofstra vs. Delaware, live on WFAN. Let me tell you something—that game was on ESPN, and nobody cared. They were more interested in the fact that Mike and Chris were there, as promised, and then we went out and won the game. It was the first time Hofstra made the NCAA tournament since '77. People were more excited that Mike and the Mad Dog were there than by us making the NCAA!

"It was the biggest thing, and I'll never forget this: I'm driving into the game for an 11:00 tip, so I'm driving in at 9:30—and they're already there! They're already on the air, from the arena, doing a Saturday morning show. They did so well, we did the same thing all over again the next year."

To many, the opinions of Russo and Francesa became the most important in New York sports.

"The biggest thing for me, growing up, was when something was going on, I always said to myself, 'What do Mike and Chris think about this?' When I would get home from school, I would always have Mike and Chris on for that reason," said Evan Roberts, an underrated radio historian and one of WFAN's midday hosts. "My favorite part of *Mike and the Mad Dog* was when there would be a baseball game on in the afternoon and they would basically be breaking down and doing play-by-play of the game as it's happening. The one that jumps out is Kerry Wood's 20-strikeout game. Cubs-Astros in '98. Wrigley Field. Because I get home from school and I put the game on TV, and I'm listening to Mike and Chris talk on WFAN as Wood pitches!"

Roberts—a huge Mets fan and not a bad impressionist, either—then does his best Mad Dog.

"Hey, take a look at Kerry Wood here, Michael. He has a chance today." That's when they were at their best. That team probably had the best chemistry of any radio duo in the history of the business. I don't think anybody could ever match it. I would hate them equally at times. When Mike would talk about the Yankees and all their championships and the Mets were kind of the little guy in '98, '99, 2000, I wanted to choke Mike. I loved him but I wanted to choke him, because as a Mets fan I was like, 'Oh god, here he is with the Yankees again. Ugh.' Even Dog, who you'd want to stand up for the Mets, always hated the Mets. They're playing the Giants in the play-offs and he's going nuts.

"So I loved them and hated them at times. But I always listened. You *had* to."

The rest of New York did, too, right from the get-go. While the two hosts were still figuring out their chemistry, the city went along for the ride. If there were issues internally, they were invisible to the listeners.

"Well, it worked pretty well close to the beginning, over the air. Whoever might have thought cynically about it on Day 1 probably would have been warming up to it by Day 5," Rose said. "It just seemed to be one of those things from the outset that was so zany that even though it had every reason to fail, it would more than likely succeed."

And as it did, Francesa and Russo became celebrities. In and outside of the station, even in a day and age when people didn't recognize most radio hosts on the street, these guys were getting enough press to break through those barriers. Where Franklin tried so hard—probably too hard—and failed to become the king of New York, these guys were sharing the throne with relative ease. It never seemed, on the air, as if what they were doing was difficult.

"And it wasn't, let's be honest here," Russo said, simply. "Two guys talking sports, having a good time on the radio. It's not like we were trying to split an atom there."

"Chris' knowledge was always knocked, but Chris definitely knows what's going on. He pays closer attention than people give him credit for," said Spitz. "And the entertainment piece of it when those two went at it? It was off the charts.

"I never produced their show on a regular basis. I worked with both of them separately and produced Mike's *NFL Now* show for a number of years. I worked closer with Chris on *In the Huddle*, when he and [former New York Jets quarterback and eventual WFAN morning show host] Boomer Esiason had the NFL show together, and I was sort of the backup when their main producers were out. But I was never far from them. There was something special when you heard that theme song with the two of them going at it. And the strength was it was all real. There was nothing phony about it."

Oh, that song. The unforgettable, unmistakable jingle that many a New York sports fan can repeat to this day:

"Mike...and...the Mad Dog...Sports Radio 66, W-F-A-N! They're talking sports, going at it as hard as they can! It's Mike and the Mad Dog on The Fan. Nothing can get by them, turn it on and try them. Mike and the Mad Dog, W-F-A-N!"

"Aaaaaaaaaaaaaaaaaaaaaaaaaaaaaaaaaand good afternoon, everybody! How are you today? The *Mike and the Mad Dog* radio program. Nice to have you with us on this Tuesday, the 30th day of November, 1999. As we talk about the world of sports, 718-937-6666 is your two-way sports talk telephone number. Lot to get to today, on this busy Tuesday. And good afternoon there, Michael, how are you?"

"I'm fine Dog, and..."

And just like that, on seemingly every weekday afternoon, all of New York sports centered around two figures in a studio talking to each other—and to all of us at the same time.

"I think what makes them stand out—to guests and callers alike—is that when you got on with them, you could always, *always* just be yourself. Because that's what *they* were doing, being themselves," Wright said. "The bottom line for me is that I'll always know they helped me at Hofstra. Because I'm telling you, we were awful, and they still had me on and pumped us up."

Keep in mind, this is a coach who led Villanova to the 2009 Final Four and now has 10 NCAA tournament bids—and counting—under his belt.

"Back then at Hofstra, doing those shows, I only had one thing going for me: that I was a regular on *Mike and the Mad Dog*. So, after that, at Villanova, doesn't matter. They could kill me about anything—tough loss, upset—I'd go along with it because of what they did for me. And trust me, Mike would get on there and kill me for some losses."

Wright then did his best Francesa imitation, with a smile on his face. These two hosts seemingly inspire everyone, from all walks of life, to imitate them.

"'That's a bad, bad loss for Jay. Let's see if we can get Jay on to talk about that one, Dog.' But I could take anything they give me on the air, because I know what they did for me to get me started.

"And when I look back on it, and as coaches you do so many shows, they stand out so much because you respect their knowledge, you respect their skills. Always."

The New York Yankees and those involved with their burgeoning cable television channel—one destined to change baseball broadcasting forever—felt the same way. Not long after the turn of the century, as the Yankees Entertainment and Sports Network was plotting out its strategy, its programming, and its overall brand, the groundbreaking executives knew they needed something daily, something newsy, something New York.

The goal at YES was to be all Yankees, all of the time, and to do it in a way that didn't follow the 1980s superstation template. WTBS and WGN—where you could get tons of Atlanta Braves and Chicago Cubs games, respectively—were great. But the emphasis was on *were.* Those channels provided baseball fans with lasting memories, for sure. But at the same time, they also provided reruns of *All in the Family* and *Cheers.*

YES didn't want any part of that business model.

"We're not cookie cutter. We're never going to be cookie cutter. We didn't want to be like the other regional sports networks, so let's be different. Let's go all out. We knew that we were going to play to our Yankee audience, because 99.9 percent of the people that were going to watch this network were going to be Yankee fans. They want to know about the Yankees. So, long story short, we needed people in the afternoon who were going to talk about the Yankees."

Those were the words of one John Filippelli, the president of production and programming at YES, and a former executive vice president of the station. So much of what YES was and is today is the brainchild of this sports television mogul, and he remembers those early days of the channel as if they were last week.

Those programming meetings went something like this. "Let's do Yankees, Yankees, Yankees. And when we're not doing Yankees, let's find some other stuff that still has some Yankees flavor to it."

Mike and the Mad Dog was quintessential "other stuff."

"There's no question it was the perfect storm and it was the right time to do this. From the 1980s, they had been in place, they had already been on the air as a team 14 years by the time YES came along. So, again, there's a built-in brand there, and it was a perfect fit for us. And it was a perfect fit for them, because it was a way for them to expand their brand, get on television, and change their profiles," Filippelli recalled.

"The increased notoriety was certainly going to be good for them and WFAN. And certainly, the idea of me being able to have credible and interesting sports programming on our network was a huge plus for us."

There wasn't much to debate about on either side. Like *Imus in the Morning* on MSNBC, YES was going to plant cameras in and around the WFAN studios and catch the two sports-media giants on a daily basis from 1:00 to 6:30 PM talking New York sports.

On March 19, 2002, as the Yankees prepped for another season full of expectations after losing the World Series to the Arizona Diamondbacks the year before, the life and times of Mike and the Mad Dog changed forever.

And it played out live on YES.

"We have a new group on the board today, Mike, we're looking forward to a relationship. Nice to have everyone with us. 718-937-6666," a clean-cut Russo proclaimed to the audience. As he looked down at his desk, Russo did not make much eye contact with the YES camera on this opening-day introduction. Just seconds before Russo spoke with his sky-blue Polo button-down shirt on, he bobbed his head back and forth to the rhythm of the show's theme song, showing just a glimpse of the mannerisms and body language that would make him even more famous on television.

All the while, Francesa adjusted the watch on his left wrist and dusted off the left sleeve of his jet-black sport coat, almost like a batter going through some on-deck rituals before entering the box.

"Well, 14 years later, the *Mike and the Mad Dog* show takes a new little twist, and that is simulcast on the YES Network, which we know you've heard about in the last couple of months and has been discussed, obviously, everywhere," Francesa said. "Part of that is that Dog and I would come along and be part of it...every day.

"And away we go."

No longer was *Mike and the Mad Dog* something for your ears. It was now something for your eyes as well, and it added, almost instantaneously, to the celebrity that they had built in the Big Apple. Francesa and Russo were already stars when the new network began broadcasting that spring. But as the YES channel took root, and more and more television sets were fixated on that small studio in Astoria for five and a half hours a day, they were becoming *superstars*.

With that came more pressure to perform, to produce, to dazzle—at all times. It was still radio, of course. But things had changed.

"It doesn't make it as spontaneous as it was. You have to be a little more cautious, careful about everything," Russo said. "It also changes the dynamics of how you do a show. You can't eat on the air. You can't yawn on the air. Can't do the normal things that—five hours every day—you might end up doing when you don't have TV cameras in front of you. It does change. It puts you on guard a little more than normal. And by putting you on guard a little more than normal, it takes away a little of the spontaneity of the show.

"You gain some things, of course. You gain some notoriety. Probably helps you get a guest or two. When you bring a guest in, it's nice to have them on camera. But you lose a little flexibility because you can't do as many remotes. You have to be careful; they have to go with you, everywhere you go. So you have to be sure they're allowed to bring their cameras to where you are going.

"But it was big then, for us and the station. It's almost now become the norm. But we were probably the first ones to do it for sports radio."

Before the show made its TV debut, there was much speculation in the tabloids about how the duo would play on the Yankees' network. Francesa, of course, was a Yankees fan. Russo, of course, was not. Would Francesa favor the Bronx Bombers too much on the team's own station? Would Russo go the opposite way?

"Well, we talked about that up front," Filippelli said. "In the contract, we put in there that there was no editorial control. I have editorial control over everything on this network. We have editorial control over the Yankees, too. But it was stipulated from the beginning that we had no editorial control over whatever they [Mike and Chris] were going to say or do. We knew who they were. I knew they were extremely opinionated. You don't distinguish yourself by having milquetoast opinions or just reading scores. You've got to engage your audience and you've got to be able to fascinate your audience. You've got to be able to enrage your audience and you've also got to be able to entertain your audience. And those guys could do all those things. They didn't need me to teach them to do what they did. They did what they did extremely well.

"So, if there was a time when Bernie Williams was in a 3-for-30 slump? Well, they were going to get on Bernie Williams for being in a 3-for-30 slump. There wasn't much I could do about it."

There was enough mutual respect between all parties—the network, the Yankees, and Russo and Francesa—to be smart about all of that anyway. The show was still going to be the same show that had made the hosts stars, cameras or not, but there was a healthy sense of professionalism present. There was too much admiration for Yankees owner George Steinbrenner—and the enormity of the endeavor, for that matter—to push the envelope too far.

"The simulcast is an enormous part of our success. And it's ironic because it started in the most unusual way. FAN was negotiating. CBS was negotiating a contract with the Yankees. And George Steinbrenner was in the midst of starting the YES Network. And he made it clear that he wanted *Mike and the Mad Dog* as a simulcast to be part of the contract," Francesa said. "It was actually George Steinbrenner who came up with the idea to simulcast *Mike and the Mad Dog*. Give him credit for that. Whether it was George himself or somebody whispering in George's ear, I can't answer, but I know I was confronted by executives who said 'George Steinbrenner is adamant that *Mike and the Mad Dog* be on YES.' He wrote it into the radio deal. And that's how it started. They had already done it.

"When it was done that way—they came to us after the deal was already done and said 'All right, what do you want?'—at that point, we had to decide. And we were like 'We're basically going to do this show, our show, but we're going to let them eavesdrop.' That's how we thought of it. One of the things we decided early on was, we were not going to play to the TV cameras. Yes, we were going to pitch some stuff in there and sometimes address YES, and sometimes address TV. 'Look at this replay' and stuff. But often we were just going to let the cameras eavesdrop on what we did.

"I took that idea from watching the old show *The Sportswriters on TV*, which was an early show that was on SportsChannel years and years ago. It was out of Chicago. They just used to start the show cold. They'd be talking as the cameras came into the room and you would leave as the cameras would pull out, and they'd still be talking. I said, 'That's the right way to do it. Just eavesdrop.' YES accentuates some different things, and they've done a great job with that. But I'll tell you this: you can't separate *Mike and the Mad Dog*'s success, my success, from the simulcast.

"The simulcast gave us a national audience. It changed everything. *Mike and the Mad Dog* is historic in a couple ways. That was one of them."

Filippelli, along with so many others, concurs.

"Some of the great moments in the network have been from them. That is not lost on me or anyone here," he said with conviction and pride. "I'm sure the same thing can be said for WFAN, as well."

Not bad for a couple of Pete Franklin substitutes, and a pairing that was more whim than wisdom nearly three decades ago.

"Well, we gave it a shot," Smulyan said with a laugh. "I guess it worked out."

4

The Battle of Midday

It's a tough slot, yes, but I just enjoyed the job. I didn't really think about it. It's like baseball. One thing I learned about baseball: baseball guys, and many guys in pro sports, say, 'Hey, control what you can control.' So we did that. Everything else, that was out of our realm. Ratings, that stuff, you just can't control, I don't think. Particularly in that time slot. Morning and afternoon drive? Sure, you can be more hands-on and have more of an effect. Unless you're giving away cash, you're not going to have that big of an effect on midday. It's just one of those 'is what it is' situations.   —DAVE SIMS

ART RUST JR. NEVER MADE IT TO THE FAN, but he had an influence on a good number of hosts who did. Rust, a New York native born in Harlem, held numerous roles across many platforms in the Big Apple, but the one that stands out, the one that inspired so many others, was his gig as the host of a little radio show in the early 1980s called *Sportstalk*.

Rust, a grizzled veteran of print, television, and radio, attacked many a sports topic on the pioneer of a show for WABC. There was no WFAN back in 1981, obviously, and the doomed project that was Enterprise Radio was scuffling to find its way over in the rolling hills of Connecticut. For a good long while in the sports radio stratosphere, there was Rust...and that was it.

WABC, 770 on your AM dial, was nowhere near an all-sports format at the time. That wasn't even on its radar. It was a Top 40 station in 1981, playing the likes of "Bette Davis Eyes" by Kim Carnes, "Jessie's Girl" by Rick Springfield, and "I Love a Rainy Night" by Eddie Rabbitt.

Who needs sports radio when you've got Eddie Rabbitt? On crystal-clear AM no less?

Well, in 1982, the station ditched the hits and changed its format. Plenty of news. Plenty of talk. And just a little touch of sports. Which is where Rust, an African American who died in 2010 at the age of 82, upped his profile, filling some time talking Mets, Yankees, Giants, Jets, Knicks, and Nets with the people of the city. For that time period, it worked. It wasn't spectacular radio, but it was *different*, if nothing else. And many took notice.

Dave Sims was one of them. Himself an African American working as a sportswriter at the *New York Daily News*, Sims enjoyed Rust's opinions, appreciated the insight, and was honored to often be an on-air guest.

"I listened to Art a lot when I was at the *Daily News*, and I don't remember how the heck we met. But then the next thing I know, I was on there a lot, and I loved it. Lot of fun," Sims said with a laugh and smile that is seen at every baseball game he broadcasts now for the Seattle Mariners, among other on-air gigs. "I was the first black sportswriter at the *Daily News*, and there haven't been a heck of a lot after me. But that was pretty cool to do that [with Art]. It was like being with an uncle for me because Art's reference points were a carbon copy of my old man's. So we hit it off really well."

Along the way, Sims, a Philadelphia native who was still easing his way into life some 90 miles up the road in the Big Apple, found that he was pretty good on the air himself—opinionated, thorough, and funny. And soon enough, others noticed. Halfway through the decade, WNBC, which took residence at 660 AM before the switch to WFAN, hired the affable Sims and gave him his own time slot. *SportsNight* was a call-in show that crossed five hours, spanned the globe of sports, and ran right up against, yep, Art Rust Jr.

"I went from frequent guest on Art's show to having a show going against him, so that was a riot," Sims said, chuckling. "And the fact that we had two black guys, one a generation older, was great. Art had to be a good 20 years older than I am, but it was an interesting generation span, having two black guys in New York City on 50,000-watt blowtorches talking sports. I thought that was huge. I don't think anybody's said a lot about that. But given where this country is and where it came from, we always thought that was pretty damn significant. It was a lot of fun."

So, as listeners and callers alike began to warm toward Sims' solo act, he seemed like a perfect fit for The Fan, the empire still under construction. It seemed like a matter of time before his wit and wisdom found a new home, and in the 1990s, he finally did. Sims was hired for a show with partner Ed Coleman.

It was to be the midday show, the dreaded 10:00 AM to 1:00 PM hole after *Imus in the Morning* and before *Mike and the Mad Dog*. It was a tough spot to be in, attempting to bridge the gap between the station's two tentpoles. People weren't driving *to* work at that time, as they were during Imus. And people weren't driving home *from* work at that time, like they were during Francesa and Russo. The midday was kinda just…there.

But Sims had already overcome a lot in his day. What was another challenge to a guy like him? Like Rust, Sims was persistent, passionate, and proud. In other words, he was perfect for tackling that midday melancholy.

"We just wanted to put on a quality program," Sims said simply. And they did.

The show was named *The Coleman and the Soul Man*, and the pair was fair with callers, booked plenty of guests, and shared many a laugh along the way. In a Bermuda Triangle of a time slot, Coleman and Sims swam along with the swirling tides just fine.

The Coleman and the Soul Man was a different type of program, and that was par for the course in terms of WFAN's approach to the midday. You have to stand out, you always have to be thinking ahead. And regardless of the management team in place during different eras of The Fan, none of them ever threw their hands up and gave up on that time slot. There was always something new, something bold, to try.

None bigger than two out-of-towners trying to make a midday dent in the media capital of the world.

"In retrospect, I learned they wanted me to be the ugly black man, the angry black man, and Eddie was going to be the cool and calm guy from Boston. They figured there'd be sparks flying! The white, Irish guy from Boston, and a black guy from Philly! 'This is going to be combustible.' Turns out, we hit it off beautifully," Sims said proudly. "We dug each other immediately. A lot of people said it created boring radio, but I said it was great conversational radio. That was one of the beauties of The Fan: If you wanted sparks and confrontation and this, that, and the other thing, in terms of explosiveness, you had Mike and Chris later on. But Eddie and I, for the most part, we got along great."

Coleman, with as many laughs as Sims had in his response, concurred.

"It's funny, I've always thought of Philly and Boston as big towns. And New York is a city. To me, there aren't that many cities. Boston was very much a big town. Philly is kind of the same way. Dave always looked at it that way and we hit it off, based on that," Coleman said. "It was a lot of fun working with him. And we agreed with a lot of our hits and misses."

There's always going to be a few of the latter.

"We had a show at [the now-closed] Mickey Mantle's [Restaurant] that we loved doing down there [in Manhattan]. One of my idols in sports—and I think Dave's, too—has always been Willie Mays. So we're fortunate enough one time at Mickey Mantle's to have him on the show...and he couldn't have been more of a jerk that day," Coleman added, laughing in retrospect. "If he's not in the mood to do something that day, you know it and we knew it. But it's funny, when Willie left near the end of the show, Dave and I looked at each other and said, 'I can't believe how much of an asshole he was.'"

Coleman later recalled a warmer story about meeting up with Mays in San Francisco, when the former was on assignment covering the Mets for WFAN in 1996. Coleman had to fly home unexpectedly after hearing the news of his mother's death from cancer, some two years after he lost his father. As Coleman was waiting for the taxi to take him to the airport, he was greeted by Mays.

"Willie came out and spent about 15 minutes with me until the cab came, just talking about life, about his parents. It was great. I saw another side of him at that point and realized that's why I liked him so much as a ballplayer," Coleman said. "I always thought Willie was the best all-around ballplayer I ever saw. I grew up watching Ted Williams. And as a kid, when Ted Williams was playing, he was the greatest hitter I ever saw. I was a Red Sox fan growing up, but Willie was the best all-around player I ever saw.

"I just thought it was funny. Dave and I were both kind of surprised at that interview. I thought it was going to be a really good time. And it was like the worst of all. Turns out, he was just probably having a bad day. But it goes back to us being on the same page. Dave and I were just like that."

"I think we had one significant argument about [former Mets manager] Davey Johnson," Sims said. "I thought Davey Johnson could change his stripes and he didn't think so. We got into a long and what turned out to be an extraordinarily stupid debate about whether or not he could change coming off a couple poor seasons before he got fired. It was entertaining, if nothing else."

And that's what the midday show has been for years at The Fan. Long-lasting? No. Headline-grabbing? Not always. Revenue-generating? Eh.

But always entertaining, always unique, and always forward thinking.

• • •

Russ Salzberg is a television sports anchor on WWOR Channel 9 who formed an identity on the air that dovetailed with his wardrobe. Known for wearing colorful sweaters on camera—not unlike the ones that former St. John's basketball coach Lou Carnesecca wore on the sideline at Madison Square Garden—and using catchphrases during highlights—"Bye-bye, so long, farewell" is his home-run call—Salzberg teamed up with Steve Somers for their own midday whirl.

"When we were doing it, Steve and I ended up doing pretty good," Salzberg said. "At one point, we got as high as No. 2 [in the ratings]. I don't know if anybody has been No. 2 since then. I'm not saying they haven't, I'm saying that I don't know. But I know we got as high as No. 2."

Somers was already stitched into the fabric of WFAN, having climbed up the ladder from being the overnight host. "Under the covers, schmoozing some S-P-O-R-T-S on The Fan, New York City," Somers was indeed known as "the Schmoozer," among many other monikers, and he developed an overnight family, a legion of callers and guests, and took ownership of the shift that seemingly no one ever wanted. His patented slow delivery, his unmistakably professional treatment of his callers, and his unforgettable opening monologues will live forever in the annals of WFAN history.

Always looking to make a splash, the station decided to give this parlay a ticket to the midday dance in the 1990s. Their show was dubbed *The Sweater and the Schmoozer*, and just like that, a new late-morning, early-afternoon team took the field.

"The funny thing was [former sales and general manager] Joel Hollander wanted to hook me up with [*Daily News* columnist] Mike Lupica to do a midday show and it was all set to go, but there was a changeover [in WWOR management]," Salzberg said. "The news director at the time was fired and the new guy coming in, quite frankly, became a very good ally of mine and a supporter of me. But there was a transition period, and because of that transition period with the new guy coming into the station, all a sudden, they didn't want me to do the radio. So I couldn't do it.

"Then less than six months later, the news director came to me and said, 'Hey, go ahead and do it.' At that point I called [WFAN] up and said, 'Just so you know, if you want to do this again I'm ready to do it.' Next thing you know, they put me in with Steve Somers."

The result wasn't spectacular, wasn't legendary, and often didn't maintain the audience from Imus to Francesa and Russo like it needed to. But it wasn't awful radio, either. You had two opinionated voices—very deep-rooted in the sports culture of New York—who knew the station's philosophies and intentions.

Sometimes, though, those talented voices fail to mesh. Whether it was Salzberg—who did solo shows before Somers was added as his partner—being more used to TV, or Somers being more suited for the overnight, there was something missing. The chemistry wasn't there.

"First of all, you have to know what your audience is," Salzberg said. "To me, somebody sitting at home between 10:00 AM and 1:00 PM is not the same as the guy driving to work in the morning or the guy in the afternoon driving home. There were a couple of things in play in my view. Number one, just from my point of view, I had a good relationship with pretty much all of the teams and a great deal of the players and managers and coaches and general managers and owners. The problem was, between 10:00 and 1:00, for example, the Knicks were pretty much practicing or busy during that time period, so that derailed us from getting them on the show. In '94 and '95, you talk about hockey and basketball in its heyday here—the Rangers, the Devils. A lot of those guys aren't available at that time. Football, a lot of those guys weren't available at that time."

WFAN has since addressed that problem to some extent, orchestrating independent deals with players to appear on shows weekly for financial considerations.

"I see people today and I kind of giggle," Salzberg said. "I only wish Steve and I had paid guests who you can count on to come on. They're coming on because it's a *paid gig*! When you get someone paid to come on, you know they're coming on. You don't have to worry about it."

Still, though, *The Sweater and the Schmoozer* battled on.

"That said, we had [George] Steinbrenner on all the time, got a lot of guys on. But it was work. And the other thing was—it might not have been for everybody—but Steve and I had our schtick. It was indeed *The Sweater and the Schmoozer,* and we'd laugh and do our schtick and have our arguments. During midday, you need some of that stuff.

"Now there are iPhones, there's the Internet, there are all kinds of things that made it change. More people can listen through more formats and I'm sure that helps that time slot. But at that juncture, for us, it was the radio. That's what it was. The world has changed."

Not unlike the midday slot itself. Across the span of The Fan, in no particular order, there have been as many hosts, it seems, as there have been coaches for the Knicks.

Lupica and Len Berman, the latter a television sports anchor like Salzberg, agreed to take up the slot once, but the show never took to the air. Berman had second thoughts, knowing his commitments at WNBC Channel 4 already took up a good portion of his days. He didn't feel he could make the entire time slot, so WFAN broke up the pair, and gave Lupica 10:00 AM to noon and Berman noon to 2:00 PM.

It wasn't meant to be in the end. Maybe the shows were too short to gain any following. Maybe they couldn't hold listeners' attention for very long. Either way, both shows soon went the way of other midday experiments: into the trash.

• • •

That doesn't mean WFAN stopped trying. After *The Sweater and the Schmoozer* had run its course, Suzyn Waldman, a former update anchor and the first voice ever heard on WFAN, teamed up with Jody McDonald, a former overnight host, for their turn behind the mic. Waldman was the former WFAN beat reporter for the Yankees, and McDonald's father, Joe, was a former general manager of the Mets. This pairing had potential; there was certainly a wealth of sports knowledge and plenty of experience on both sides. But when talking about the midday malaise, something always seemed to foil the best-laid plans.

"I love Suzyn. I think she's great at what she does now [as radio analyst for the Yankees] and she was a pretty darn good talk show host partnered with me," McDonald said. "But you talk about groundbreaking and being the first and the like, well, Suzyn was the first female full-time, major-market, midday talk show host. Nobody had ever done anything like that before.

"I was trying to strike the balance as best we could and I think we did a pretty good job of it. I enjoyed working with her on a day-in, day-out basis. I think we did it for a year and change—into November or December the year after we started in May. And Suzyn just didn't like the politics of it, deciding what to do on a day-in and day-out basis, the discrepancies on whether we should lead with hockey or basketball or football or baseball. She had been a reporter all her life and that meant being out on the road and not being locked in a studio every day.

"What she told me was she just didn't like the repetition of it, the overseeing of all of it. She resigned."

Waldman, in 2001, received an unrivaled opportunity to work for the Yankees Entertainment and Sports Network. She left WFAN just before that, did reporting for YES, and eventually worked her way up to her current role as the team's radio commentator.

"I definitely missed her when she left," McDonald said bluntly.

But opportunity knocks, and Waldman's exit opened another door for Sidney Ferris Rosenberg. Life in the midday—and for McDonald—would never be the same.

"Sid was fun. Sid was funny. Sid was nuts. He brought energy every single day," McDonald summarized. "What a ride."

Rosenberg was a New York bolt of lightning who feared no guest, no topic, and no caller. After ingraining himself into the culture of

WFAN as the sports-update man on *Imus in the Morning,* he was becoming a seasoned sports-radio professional despite his lack of an accredited education in the business.

He was bold. He was brash. He was Brooklyn. And when you added it all up, he was perfect as McDonald's next partner.

"He was bouncing off the walls at all times," McDonald said, "which is good because he could pick me up on days when I needed a pick-me-up. You never had to worry about that with Sid. With Sid, it was more trying to calm him down, because he didn't always stay focused and he would, at times, go off on a tangent.

"He had the best energy I've seen of anybody I've worked with in radio. But sometimes his energy would be a deterrent and would take us off to places where we necessarily didn't have to go. It was always fun with Sid. I wouldn't trade the time for anything in the world but it was work. It was management because Sid was a little crazy, both on and off the air."

Rosenberg, who has fought demons his whole career and has paid the price personally and professionally, will attest to that. Sometimes, whether he was going off on one of those "tangents" on air or out celebrating another quality show at a New York establishment, Sid just didn't know when to stop.

But that was his brand, his identity, and what put him in the position he was in at WFAN, misgivings notwithstanding. As the update man for Imus, Rosenberg took the ball, ran it down the field, through the end zone, into the tunnel, past the locker room, out to the Meadowlands parking lot, and off to the New Jersey Turnpike. He was New York's version of Forrest Gump—"Run, Rosenberg, Run!"—and he just never, ever stopped.

"For me, I had nothing to lose," Rosenberg said. "Patrick McEnroe was already a tennis star on ESPN [when he was the Imus update man]. Mike Breen was already doing Knicks games [when he was the

Imus update man]. So while Breeny did some really, really great stuff, creative stuff, songs and all that good stuff, he couldn't go on and talk about lesbians and he couldn't go on and do the crazy things I was doing. He had something to lose. I had nothing to lose. I was a guy who, five years prior, was in rehab, and three years prior was waiting on tables in a seafood restaurant in a mall in Boca Raton, Florida!

"To me, I was playing with house money. I was new. It wasn't like I was going to destroy my reputation or ruin my career. I was the new guy on the block and was trying to make a name for myself. When I think back now, it was actually pretty selfish, because I did have plenty to lose: I had my job to lose, my reputation, I hurt my wife and my family, and to this day, there are people in my family who are upset with some of the things that are said and written about me.

"WFAN was giving me an opportunity to become a household name and I was going to do it, and make Imus *that* guy people were talking about again."

Well, they eventually started talking about Rosenberg, too. And sensing his rising stardom, believing that maybe there was more there than simply being one of Imus' minions, WFAN management made him a battery mate with McDonald. Before too long, the former Florida waiter who got his start with an Internet radio company in the Sunshine State before parlaying that into a gig at WNEW 102.7 FM in New York, was smack dab in the middle of WFAN's broadcast day. Not a bad career path, all things considered.

"[Manager of operations] Mark Chernoff really thought I could do it," said Rosenberg, who didn't need to leave WNEW but found the potential at WFAN too great to ignore. "The issue was I was making a six-figure salary doing mornings at WNEW and there were no big slots available at WFAN. They had *Imus in the Morning*, they had Jody and Suzyn, they had Mike and Chris, and I couldn't make six figures at WFAN. I had a family, a wife, and bills, and I couldn't just do weekends and fill-ins, so I was going to have to leave it be.

"It was Mark Chernoff who thought I had so much promise. And he liked me so much—and again, I was so wet behind the ears—he said to me, 'Listen, Imus needs that guy to give a little more spunk in the mornings, so we'll throw you on with Imus.'

"You have to understand, when I was a kid going to Poly Prep in Brooklyn, that's all my dad listened to: Imus. That's it. So I heard Imus for years as a kid."

Chernoff also laid the foundation for Rosenberg's midday show entrance.

"Chernoff said, 'They're about to start a new network up here, which no one knows about, for the Yankees,'" Rosenberg recalls. "'As soon as they start that network, Suzyn is gone. And the day that she's gone, I promise you, if you stick around and work with Imus and do weekends and do what I think you can do, I'll put you on with Jody.'"

Indeed, with the creation of YES, Waldman said good-bye to The Fan, and it seemed quite apropos. In the end, she was a perfect fit for her new gig, and her departure meant that a midday microphone was now open.

"Chernoff said this to me four months before it all went down," Rosenberg said. "'For a chance to stay in New York and work at The Fan, I'll do it,' I said. It was difficult because my wife was still living in Florida and I had to travel back and forth, literally, on weekends just to go see her. And I did it. I started doing sports on *Imus*. I did a couple of weekend shifts. I filled in for [Joe] Benigno on overnights every now and again just to make ends meet. And eventually, three or four months later, everything Chernoff said came to fruition. Suzyn went to the YES Network, and sure enough I had my midday slot with Jody McDonald. I was back to making six figures and it was all okay.

"Four months later, I was doing *Imus*, I was doing middays, and soon after that, I was doing pregame for the Giants. Nobody owned more real estate per minute on WFAN than me, which was pretty amazing considering three years before that, I was a waiter at a seafood restaurant in Boca Raton."

But there were errors in judgment, and it's tough to undo those on radio, as he's quick to point out now. In talking once about the first family of women's tennis, Rosenberg suggested that Venus and Serena Williams might want to consider posing in *National Geographic* instead of *Playboy*.

He later took aim at the potentially debilitating physical appearance of pop singer Kylie Minogue, a 1980s superstar who was battling breast cancer after a comeback brought her back to relevance in the U.S. in the 2000s.

Both of those comments were made on *Imus* but the effects were felt everywhere, including the midday show. It's difficult to bounce back from those, and while it's true that radio must go on, it doesn't always go on easily.

Maybe some of those mistakes could have been avoided if he didn't overdo it on Imus' show in the interest of standing out. Perhaps there was an Imus Sid, so to speak, as well as a Sports Sid.

"I became a mouthpiece and I was all too willing to do it. I just wanted to make him happy and get my name out there," Rosenberg said of Imus. "And it didn't work and I suffered the consequences. By the way, to this day I still have difficulty getting certain jobs and certain people will never, ever give me any credibility because of the things I did and said on Imus in an attempt to make him happy and make the show something people talked about at the water cooler every single day.

"To this day, people are still not able to separate the character I was on Imus and who I really am."

On the midday show with McDonald, though, listeners heard snippets of a different Sid. A true, hardcore New York sports fan, one with an encyclopedic memory, Rosenberg—who later teamed up with Benigno, the converted caller-slash–overnight host, after McDonald left—found his footing in that middle position. And like other born-and-bred New Yorkers on the air, he formed a sincere bond with the WFAN callers. Even if he was making his point so fast, so fiercely, that you couldn't always understand it.

"I think if Sid was doing a talk show in New York, whether he's doing one in Florida, whether he's doing one in Australia, whether he's baking bread, whether he's running a company, I think Sid's Sid," McDonald said when asked if the sudden fame of being at WFAN got to Rosenberg. "I think it's just his personality and I think he would be the same, no matter what, no matter how big his star was, or how insulated his star was. I don't think it would make him be a different guy. I think that's his personality and it's contagious, it's outrageous, and at times it's addictive...which is a problem."

Indeed. Drugs, alcohol, and gambling have all crept their way into Rosenberg's life and have often sidetracked his career. In 2005, after problems both off and on the air at WFAN, his time there came to an end.

But his talent and his passion for the industry often rises above everything else, wherever he goes. Not unlike troubled athletes who get second chances in the NFL or NBA after lapses in judgment, there aren't a lot of hosts out there who can do what Rosenberg does. As a result, Rosenberg usually finds a way to find work.

WAXY-AM 790 in Miami gave him a chance as a morning host. Later, South Florida's WQAM-AM 560 gave him an afternoon gig. At WQAM, his demons resurfaced.

On April 5, 2012, he was charged with driving under the influence, a charge that was later dismissed. It was that incident—which perhaps gained more notoriety than the others because of an alarming mug shot that was tweeted and retweeted worldwide—that may have led to Rosenberg turning a corner.

"Every day is a new day. I feel good about myself now," Rosenberg said in a November 29, 2012, interview. "In the past, I did a lot of things for other people. I tried to get healthy for my wife because I don't want to lose her. I tried to get healthy for Chernoff because I didn't want to lose my job at The Fan. I would always try to get healthy for the wrong reasons. This is the first time I said, 'For me, it's enough.' Nobody put a gun to my head. There wasn't a court order. My wife didn't tell me to get out. None of that stuff went down.

"And when you do it for yourself, that's when everyone else reaps the rewards. That's the first thing people need to know, anyone who's got any issue. When they go and get help and do it for everybody else but them, they're doing it for all the wrong reasons. If you start to get help for anything that's going wrong in your life and you're doing it for *you*, that's the first real shot you've got."

In August of 2012, a rejuvenated Rosenberg—who has done part-time work for WFAN since his full-time exit eight years ago—returned to the Florida airwaves once again, with a new morning show on WMEN-AM 640. He was grateful for the opportunity and he was doing his best to make the most of it, rolling with the punches, offering up plenty of Brooklynese, and above all else, just having some on-air fun...one day at a time.

"Thank God, I'm sober now for eight months and I'm doing great. My personal life is terrific. I never worry a day. As long as I do a good job and do the right things off the field, then on the field, the production is going to be there," Rosenberg said.

"For the first time in my life, I'm taking the right steps to make sure that's going to be the case. But it's a one-day-at-a-time thing for me, to be honest. And based upon my career and what you've seen since I started at The Fan back in 2001, for me to tell you where I'm going to be in a year, let alone five, would be kind of silly."

Rosenberg, as he'll readily admit, has made plenty of mistakes along the way, ones that he and the people around him have paid for dearly. He has ridden a roller coaster of emotions—a constant cycle of highs and lows throughout his career—that may be unrivaled, even in an industry filled with troubled souls.

But it's precisely that night-and-day past that makes him befitting of the midday role. After all, both this time slot and this person are similar, aren't they? Both often get lost among the giants of the station—of the profession, even—unless something bad happens.

And with Rosenberg, "bad" happened a lot. But as the midday has persevered, so, too, has Sid. They are both still around, still going, still trying to improve.

"Keep positive. That's what I've done this time," he said, "and that's why I really, really believe—in my heart of hearts—that we'll have a conversation in five years and the message will be just as uplifting and just as positive."

For the new Rosenberg, there seemed no other way.

5

The Schmoozer

The thing that Boomer [Esiason] and I always say about Steve [Somers] is that he referenced us. He acknowledged our existence, and that really meant a lot to us. You know, a lot of guys wouldn't reference us by name, a lot of guys wouldn't talk about the new morning show once we started here, and Steve went out of his way to support us, to promote us, to talk about us on his show. And I know that Boomer and I will never forget that and we are grateful for that. We truly appreciate what he did. It was professional...and that's Steve for you. —CRAIG CARTON

STEVE SOMERS GREW UP IN THE CHILL AND THE THRILL of San Francisco, a cultural California metropolis filled with plenty of things to lay claim to, to be proud of, to take ownership in. Indeed, as the 1962 song by George Cory and Douglass Cross proclaims so eloquently, many, many people leave their heart in San Francisco.

But Somers' heart was always someplace else. Even as a youth slowly plotting out the rest of his life, this proud, passionate child raised by parents he reveres seemingly every day on the air, longed for someplace else. He craved the unknown, some 3,000 miles away.

"I started actually knowing, probably when I was 10 or 11, that I not only wanted to be a sports broadcaster but that I wanted to work in New York. It even says underneath my graduation picture in my San Francisco high school yearbook that I wanted to be a New York sportscaster," Somers said with a laugh familiar to longtime WFAN listeners. "A lot of it had to do with the [baseball] Giants moving from New York to California."

As is often the case with sports journalists, a chance meeting or an inspirational greeting helped fuel their fire and pointed them in the right direction careerwise. Somers was no different.

"As a 10-year-old, I met [baseball broadcaster] Russ Hodges—you know, he did the Bobby Thomson home run, 'the Shot Heard 'Round the World,' back in 1951. Meeting him made an impression on me," Somers said. "Listening to him on the radio when the Giants first went out to San Francisco in 1958, *that* did it. So I knew then and there that New York was for me. New York was where I wanted to go, and even then, at that age, I had the direction and the goal and the ambition to end up here."

Hodges was a baseball broadcasting icon who authored up that unforgettable call on October 3, 1951—"The Giants win the pennant! The Giants win the pennant!"—when Thomson's three-run home run ended the season for New York in classic fashion. Hodges would follow the Giants to San Francisco to continue his career, but Somers wanted to go in the opposite direction. He wanted the bright lights and the big city. And he was willing to pay his dues to get there.

"I always say to people, if you get on an airplane in San Francisco, it would take you about six hours to get to New York," he said. "It took me 23 years."

With a lot of twists and turns along the way.

"I went looking for a sports job and ended up with a high school sports show on a Top 40 radio station in San Francisco. I did radio there, learned a lot, then I got hired in San Francisco for television sports on the weekends. I was like 21, and my tour had begun," Somers said. "Then I went to Sacramento to do TV full time, Monday through Friday. That got me to Atlanta. Atlanta got me to Los Angeles. And Los Angeles is where I did sports talk radio."

Along the way, Somers made connections. He compiled contacts, he referenced them when needed, and he used them when it came time to move on. But remember, we are talking about a tough business here; Somers can certainly attest to that. He spent two and a half years out of work along his "trail," contacts notwithstanding.

After breaking into the business with some television and radio work wherever he could find it, he heard about this all-sports outfit that was being sculpted in Queens, of all places. It was perfect for him. All-sports radio? In New York? He was prepared to walk there from Northern California, if that's what the job called for.

But WFAN was his chance at so many things. Steady work, sports talk, New York City, a lifelong dream, you name it. Check, check, check, and check.

"I also did TV sports in Los Angeles on KNBC, working with Bryant Gumbel. I was part time. But I wanted to work full time," he said. "So I went back to Sacramento, which I hated doing because I was getting farther away from New York. But then my agent, who was here in New York, read about WFAN."

Life for Mr. Somers would never be the same. He and his agent threw together a resume package. WFAN—trying to secure its original lineup—was interested. The rest is history.

"It is funny how some people get in. I had to use a videotape from my television work," Somers said. "They wanted to hear an audio tape; I didn't have one. But I had a videotape...and it worked!

They hired me to do overnight. I was the last hire of the new WFAN. They didn't know what to do with the overnight—whether they would have syndicated programming, whether they would repeat the daytime programming, or whether they would have somebody live. And we begged them to hire me. Begged! And they gave in. I got hired, and here we are."

The long journey had ended. In 1987, the California Kid caught hold of his childhood goal and vowed to never let it go. Some 26 years later, he is still a man of his word.

From his overnight sessions, where he truly developed an identity in the world's largest media market, to his daytime forays in between *Imus in the Morning* and *Mike and the Mad Dog*, to his current slot in the evenings, Somers unquestionably has become part of the fabric of not only WFAN but New York sports overall.

From Day 1, Somers has been his own person with his own schtick. And from Day 1, it's always worked.

Somers is not bold and brash or outlandish just for the sake of being so. He is slow, deliberate, efficient, and effective. He has his own lingo, he has his own way with the callers, and at the top of each shift, he delivers a monologue that sets the table for his show.

"Oh my gosh, the monologues. From the beginning everybody had a personality, and Steve Somers had a *personality*," said Jim Lampley, one of the original hosts at WFAN. "I'll never forget those shows. Did you ever listen to the overnight show Steve Somers did at the beginning? One of the things I discovered there, and I had earlier discovered with some hosts and it was definitely true with Steve, was when you have that many hours to fill up on the air, you talk slowly. The fewer listeners there are, the more slowly you talk.

"And I used to have trouble sleeping. I would turn on Steve, that soothing voice, that stretching trend he was doing, the monologues, all of it, and he was stretching every vowel and making it as long as possible.

"Well, that did it for me. He would put me to sleep! I have to admit it. But he was great, and that was him. That was his style. You have to do something to fill up the time on that shift, and Steve did it so well."

Lampley probably wasn't alone in his opinion, and the great thing about Somers is that he'd laugh that off and find the positives in it. That's what Somers does. For instance, when asked—as a part of the original WFAN crew—if he felt he'd changed the radio world, he responded in kind.

"Yeah," he said, "I changed the world all right...for the worse!"

He's far too humble, of course. For going on 30 years, he has channeled his creativity into those artfully crafted monologues on yellow legal pads. Sometimes they arrive complete with a poem, sometimes with an audio clip, but always with enough Somers-ese to make each one an original. That helped him immeasurably to stand out on the overnight shift. And along the way, Somers developed a cadre of loyal callers. Some would talk about the Mets. Some would talk about the Rangers. Some would talk about the Jets. Some would talk about all three.

It didn't matter to Somers. He always gave them the time and the opportunity to speak their minds. Along the way, the overnight became something of a family affair.

"Steve is as warm of a guy as you'll ever meet. I grew up listening to Steve and so to be here at WFAN with him, it's always been an honor for me," said Marc Malusis, one of the current overnight hosts at the station. "As a listener, you have this vision of who Steve is, and you know of him through what he says on the air. But to be here, getting to meet Steve and work with Steve and really getting to know Steve, there's just so much there. He treats everyone like those callers he has. He treats everyone with respect, he admires what people do professionally, and he is truly happy to be able to work here every day."

Malusis has also produced for Somers, so perhaps no one can better illustrate what goes into each and every Somers shift.

"He's tough because he's a perfectionist. You never want to be sloppy on the air, and Steve goes about it in a different style and fashion, with his humor and his bits and busting chops and playing along with the Islanders fans or the Yankees fans and everything like that. That's part of his charm," Malusis said. "Steve was a guy, when he was doing an opening monologue and you're on the [sound] board, you have to pay attention to make sure to hit the right piece of audio at the right time. Because he wanted everything to sound perfect."

More often than not, it does. And when you turned on a Somers overnight show, he allowed you to slip into his world just for a bit. Maybe you were a college student who pulled all-nighters. Maybe you worked the graveyard shift. Maybe, like Lampley, you just couldn't sleep. Either way, Somers never starved for listeners, and if you walked into his fraternity house, it wasn't long before you were talking like one of his brothers.

Leave it to a host who had several nicknames for himself— "Captain Midnight," "the Fearless Forecaster," and "the Schmoozer" among them—to create his own dictionary, one that you probably didn't understand if you slept through the night:

Sacramento, California, a place where Somers used to work, is known as "Sacra-tomato."

The New York Islanders, the chief rival of Somers' beloved New York Rangers, are known as the "Ice-landers."

And the "Ice-landers," who have typically played in front of small home crowds the last three decades, skate in the friendly confines of the "Nassau Mausoleum," not Coliseum.

"He is definitely unique. I think it was the relationships that Steve had with his callers that I remember the most," said Steve Levy, now an anchor on ESPN's *SportsCenter* but at one time an aspiring broadcaster at WFAN who soaked up wisdom from people such as Somers. "He gave callers an overnight home, and they became something of a legion for him."

It helped that the listeners and callers were left with new memories seemingly every night. The lingo played a large role, of course. After all, it was easy for fans to play out Somers' schtick because he traditionally used so many of the same phrases over and over. Look no further than the introductions at the top of each hour.

"Well, morning to you and how you be at 1:06 and five seconds on this Monday morning on your Fan, New York City. Steve Somers here, and you there."

But before he'd jump into his main topic or even take a call, he'd continue on with his introduction. Always, he'd do his best to deflect attention away from himself. That's the Somers Way. In the middle of his opening, in fact, he'd always make a note of his producer, the engine behind the show, the one who mixed the sound, who prepared the calls, and who drove the overnight ship to its ultimate destination. Most times, that person was WFAN veteran producer Eddie Scozzare.

Somers would always have some fun with this part of the show, which eventually became a staple. When he'd call attention to his producer and where he was stationed—"Eddie Scozzare on the other side of the glass"—a quick soundbite would play questioning just who that producer was:

"*The* Eddie Scozzare?"

And Somers would respond traditionally with a famous "Ed" from New York sports lore, just for emphasis:

"No, [former New York Rangers goaltender] Eddie Mio, who do you think we're talking here?"

"*The* Eddie Scozzare?"

"No, [former New York Mets first baseman] Ed Kranepool, who do you think we're talking here?"

And then he'd continue on with his schtick, setting up another hour of fun and games.

"It's 1-718-937-6666, under the covers, schmoozing some S-P-O-R-T-S until *Imus in the Morning* at 5:30 on The Fan in…New York City!"

"Yeah, there were so many bits to the show that if you didn't listen all the time, you just didn't get," said Eric Spitz, former WFAN program director. "But that's what makes Steve Steve. He is just so original."

"The Fearless Forecaster" was another example of that ingenuity. "Fearless," as Somers refers to him, was an imaginary handicapper extraordinaire who would lay out a game, give both sides of the coin, and pick a winner by announcing the loser…if that makes sense to you. For instance, Fearless might handicap a game between the Jets and the Giants, lay out all the particulars, and predict a Giants win in a backward fashion, followed by his famous signature at the end:

"For the New York Jets…that's…a loss!"

"The Fearless…Forrrrrecaster."

And then he would just slip back into being Steve Somers again. Simple as that.

"The only thing I came to New York with was my wits about me, my sense of humor, and the Fearless Forecaster. Because I had done the Fearless Forecaster when I was 17, working in San Francisco radio when I was just getting started," Somers said. "When I was at that Top 40 radio station—doing high school sports—Fearless was created, and even [former San Diego Chargers quarterback and now CBS broadcaster] Dan Fouts remembers. He was playing high school football at the time the Fearless Forecaster was born.

"Dan Fouts remembers all the kids and all the guys on his high school team listening to the Fearless Forecaster way back when I was picking high school games. In fact, Dan was on with me one night on WFAN and I brought it up again, and he recounted how he would never want the Fearless Forecaster to appear on campus because I had predicted his school would lose a championship game...which they did not lose. Those kids were very, very upset with Fearless."

But there haven't been many people upset with Somers since.

"I was discovering—with a sense of humor and a schtick—how all of it came together for the first time. And it was a revelation," Somers said. "It was sort of like when a baby realizes he can control moving his fingers or his toes for the first time. You know when you grow up, you take all of those kinds of things for granted. But that's how it came, naturally, and with the humor, it just happened.

"But that's what happens in this business—you find things that work. I don't care who you are, whether you're Howard Stern, whether you're Mike Francesa, whether it's *Mike and the Mad Dog*—the best show WFAN has ever had—you just don't know whether you're going to succeed or not until you go out and do it. And I had no game plan at all! It was everything on the fly. I would prepare monologues, and the reason I had monologues was because I didn't think I was going to get anybody to call in the middle of the night. Nobody had ever done a sports talk show in the middle of the night. There was such an unknown to it."

As he built this underground, overnight oasis, though, Somers slowly became less of an unknown. And how could he not? He was just too unique to go unnoticed.

Jerry Seinfeld concurred. Yep, Somers even made comedians laugh. In fact, in the heyday of the classic NBC situation comedy *Seinfeld*, Jerry ran into Somers one night in Manhattan and explained to the radio host just how much of a fan he had become of the Schmoozer.

Somers, as humble and as honored a radio star as you'll ever meet, was stunned, flattered, and grateful. "The whole bit," as he likes to say.

"I do look back to the very beginning, and in those days, with no frame of reference, you just didn't know what was going to work, if anybody was going to be calling or listening, if anyone ever thought any of this would be funny," Somers said. "So, when I first ran into Jerry Seinfeld and got to know him a little bit, I asked him, 'Jerry, when you first started listening way back when, did you actually think I was *funny*?' He said, 'What attracted me to you and the program was your heart.'

"And I don't think anybody could say something more complimentary than that. Number one, he thinks I'm funny. That is wonderful, but it was the heart, he said to me, that really stood out. And it took me a while to understand what he meant. I know now that it had to do with being courteous to people calling in the middle of the night, who might have been a shut-in, who might have been all by themselves.

"Here's one thing I've learned about radio, especially in New York: it's very personal and very intimate. So when you're listening at home in the middle of the night—*especially* in the middle of the night when you might be alone—radio becomes your friend. And I was so anxious to get to know people and have them get to know me. I don't think in my lifetime had I ever been more self-revealing than I was in the middle of the night."

And even though Somers' shows—unlike some of the other mainstays at WFAN—never landed as a simulcast on a television station, it didn't stop him from gaining a profile in New York. It was his voice, of course, that was most familiar to the fans. His style, his humor, and his superb way of piloting a show also played roles. But ever so slowly his face and his image became more recognizable. When you're at a station like The Fan for parts of four decades, eventually that's bound to happen.

"Just take him to Citi Field once, and you'll know what I'm talking about."

Those are the words of Evan Roberts, a midday host who partners with Joe Benigno, and a radio protege who seemed destined to work for WFAN. A New York sports fan through and through, a tell-it-like-it-is host who represents the younger generation of both this city and this station, Roberts grew up listening to Somers. So obviously, when Roberts got his foot in the door at WFAN, he immediately sided up to the Schmoozer. It didn't take long for them to hit it off, and they remain not only colleagues but close friends as well.

One day, the two elected to take in a Mets game at Citi Field, along with Roberts' father.

"I'm the same guy that came here from San Francisco. I'm doing the same things," Somers said. "But through the years, yes, people around you act differently. When I first went to Shea Stadium in 1987, no one knew who I was. But yes, a couple years ago I went to Citi Field with Evan Roberts and his father. Evan couldn't believe how people were coming up to me and asking for autographs!"

It certainly hit home for a longtime listener.

"You always want to feel like what you're doing is appreciated by people, that's for sure," Roberts said. "Not that I didn't already know that about Steve, but that time, you could really see what he meant to people."

For many hosts, that night would have been long forgotten. Just another night where he had to shake a few hands and sign a few autographs. But Somers—surprise, surprise—took it a different way.

"I'm not on TV in any regular way, so that's why it's so surprising," he said. "But now if I go to Citi Field, it's funny, everybody knows me! And I'm not tooting a horn or walking around with a light over my head so people can see me, either. So, really, it's funny, and it's very flattering."

He's so popular these days that other hosts get confused for him. In 2013, Benigno—a permanent replacement for Somers on the overnight before becoming a celebrity himself on television and in the midday slot with Roberts—was stopped on an airplane by a passenger who asked if he was, well...

"Steve Somers? Me? Are you kidding me?" Benigno asked with a chuckle. "On wardrobe alone, I shouldn't be confused with Steve Somers! I love ya, Steve, don't me wrong. But if there's anyone at WFAN who needs a wardrobe upgrade, it's Steve Somers!"

Somers, perhaps, has elected to display his style and substance on the air, rather than sartorially. And the listeners seem to like it that way.

Like Mets fans, who appreciate his passion and admire his honesty, Somers also has a similar effect on Rangers fans. On the overnights, when "Captain Midnight" was in full swing, it was also heady times for the Broadway Blueshirts. Combine that with the fact that the team's games were still being broadcast on WFAN at the time, and you had a winning Rangers recipe.

One of the most memorable and emotional times for Somers was the spring of 1994, when the Knicks were orchestrating a run to the NBA Finals and the Rangers were on their way to winning the Stanley Cup for the first time since 1940.

California upbringing notwithstanding, Somers got swept up in the madness, and his show became something of a Rangers workshop, where fans would congregate to talk about the wins and the losses, the ups, the downs, and the all-arounds.

"If you were a die-hard Rangers fan like I was," Malusis said, "Steve's show was a must-listen."

But, as always, Somers made those shows about the callers. Keep in mind that loyalty to the Rangers is something that is passed down from generation to generation. Families are brought up in the red, white, and blue, and it becomes something of a badge of honor.

"I'll never forget a poster that I saw that day at the parade. It said it all," former Rangers defenseman Kevin Lowe said when reflecting on the 1994 celebration in Manhattan. "It was held by a little boy, and it said, I THANK YOU. AND MY FATHER THANKS YOU. AND HIS FATHER THANKS YOU.

"And I knew right then and there what it meant to so many families who have been following the Rangers through everything for all those years. When you're playing the game and the series go from one to the other, you're focused on hockey, hockey, hockey. But when you get a chance to step back, after the fact, and see things like that, it just makes it so much more special," Lowe continued.

That was not lost on Somers then...or now.

"To understand the Rangers and their fans and their relationship is truly an unbelievable thing. The Rangers and their fans transcend their sport," Somers said. "Hockey fans, and Rangers fans in particular, are limited in number compared to baseball and football, but they could care less. They are as passionate as any out there. They are number one with their hockey team, and as passionate and knowledgeable as any other fan might be. Their voice may be louder than most."

And that spring, their time had come. Somers made sure they had every opportunity to voice their approval and rejoice in the accomplishment.

"It was a combination of happiness and joy and passion and love and emotion," he said of those 1994 overnights. "What I was able to hear was the heartbeat of the Rangers fan and the heartbeat of the city to go along with it. I also felt the soul of the city."

His relationship with the callers goes well beyond 1994, though that was clearly an apex. You see, on the overnights—no matter the host—the callers become a greater ingredient to the show simply because there is more airtime to fill.

"There were no spots. Very few commercials. You had time, and you wanted to give them their time," Somers said. "I wanted to get to know them. I wanted them—the callers, the listeners, whoever was out there in the beginning—to know me. I wanted to be friends. And I still want to be friends with these people because if they're not there, I'm not here."

Eventually, as Somers continued to cultivate his craft, WFAN management felt he had overgrown the overnight. He was *that* good, and it was time for him to reach a broader audience. That meant the midday slot, where he was summoned to add a new touch to Russ Salzberg's show. The midday ratings were sagging, and rebranding that spot with Captain Midnight as a partner couldn't hurt.

It didn't work out so well. The Sweater and the Schmoozer didn't click as expected, and though ratings did rise, and the two coexisted to a certain extent, it wasn't a long-term union. The chemistry wasn't there.

"I never saw Steve struggle with the change from the overnight. His schtick was his schtick and he did it well; quite frankly, nobody did it better than him," Salzberg said. "We could have our debates and our arguments—that's what radio is with a partner. You're on for three hours and get into something you're passionate about. That's what happens.

"I'll say this about Steve—and this isn't a knock at anybody else— but nobody, nobody, nobody did the overnight better than Steve. His mannerisms, his nature, his voice, it just worked. He's creative that way. He knew how to do it. Then he brought his schtick to the midday and we bounced it off one another. Like I say, we had our bouts. We did. No question.

"But I speak to Steve. We don't speak every day, but a couple times a year, we'll call each other up, check in. He didn't have any problem in making the transition from night to day. He's not changing his act. His routine is what it is."

From the midday, Somers was shifted to the evening slot, which is where he remains as of 2013. In that role, he serves as the bridge between Mike Francesa and the overnight host when there's no primetime ballgame to be aired. And when there is an NBA, NHL, or Major League Baseball game to be broadcast, Somers traditionally will take calls before and after the contest.

But for most, when talking about Somers and memories of his shows—good, bad, indifferent—it traditionally comes back to the overnight.

"It's funny, Steve was the original Monday-through-Friday overnight host. I was the weekend overnight host. And I think there was a period of time where Steve didn't like me because either the callers made him think I was looking to take his job or he didn't like certain things that I did," said Jody McDonald, a WFAN original host who has filled many roles in a long career that has spanned New York, Philadelphia, and national satellite radio. "But I had the distinct impression that Steve didn't like me. I wasn't looking for his job. I liked my little weekend gig. I wasn't looking to take his position, I wasn't going to move into a daytime part. I did what I ended up doing...which was leave town and get a daytime part somewhere else.

"Over the years, I became a lot more friendly with Steve. And as soon as I wasn't doing the weekend overnights anymore, he and I got along really well. Whenever I'd see him, we'd shoot the breeze. He is as unique a talk show host as you're going to find. He is a one-and-only, and if you like the way he does things, he's got a chance to be your favorite on the entire planet. If you don't like him, if you don't get him, well, you're never going to like him, never going to get him, because he never changes and he does it exactly the same. Those that love him, love him to death. And I appreciate Steve and I like him, but it's funny because I got the distinct impression when he and I were doing the same time shift—only at different days of the week—he was not my biggest fan."

Somers, though, has plenty of fans around the station nowadays, and their memories are often as sharp as his.

"Other than Mark Chernoff and Steve Somers, no one else at the radio station thought we'd be successful," said Craig Carton, who together with Boomer Esiason replaced *Imus in the Morning* with a different show that featured more sports, more guests, and maybe even more laughs than its predecessor. *Boomer & Carton* indeed was a risk that could have backfired for Chernoff and Co. But Somers, for one, knew that it wouldn't.

"We obviously were coming in with a much different type of show," Carton said, "but Steve believed in us. We'll never forget that."

Nor will Somers.

"I wish my mother and my father could hear that, too. And I know they would have been proud," he said. "I'm like that with everybody here in terms of welcoming in people. And you're right, Craig Carton came on the air with me [in 2013] and we talked about that. That means a lot to me. Whether you're an intern or whether you're the morning show hosts, I'll do that because the business is full of people who think what we're doing is more important than anything else, and they get carried away a little bit with the ego. And we all have an ego. I have an ego, too, by the way. I can feel good about myself, some shows. Other times, I feel awful because I think I've been terrible; a monologue didn't work or I gave some wrong stat or fact or information. I go home and it just kills me. It affects my appetite.

"I still care a great deal about what I do, and I care about the people around me at the station, too."

And while so much has changed at WFAN through the years, Somers is the same as he's always been. His time slots have changed, the studios have changed, and even the ways you listen to him now—iPhones, iPads, AM, FM, "the whole bit"—have changed, but Steve is still Steve, talking some "S-P-O-R-T-S on The Fan, New York City!"

"People ask me, 'Do you feel like retiring?' I always ask them, 'How do you retire from talking?' I mean, I'm like the Jamie Moyer of radio now," said Somers, referring to the veteran pitcher who became the oldest player to win a game in Major League Baseball history in 2012, when he pitched for the Colorado Rockies at 49 years old. "I don't have the same fastball I had 25 years ago, but with off-speed stuff, I can get by; get a couple people out every now and then, if you know what I mean. I can still perform okay. But for the most part you have to be good and you do have to be lucky. In this business, you generally hear when you screw up."

He certainly hasn't heard that much. And keep in mind we're talking about a pro who turned 66 on April 17, 2013.

"I haven't changed a lot. I like to stick with what works, and I always feel fortunate to have a job," he added. "I will never forget what it was like to be out of work for two and a half years. I was very, very lucky to have gotten hired here as their last hire, and I like to think what I'm doing works, so I'll keep doing it.

"My lifestyle, I think, is the same. I'm still living in the same apartment I was when I first moved here. Of course, it's a little different. I'm an old man now, not a kid. You change as you grow older but you're still the same person," Somers said. "Today, Mark Chernoff said to me, 'Your monologue yesterday was very, very funny.'

"I said, 'I didn't think it was that good, so you have to be a little bit lucky.'

"And Chernoff said to me what I've always said: 'All of us are lucky.' You have to be good and you really have to be lucky for a chance to be great. I'm glad I had the chance today...and I'll have the chance tomorrow."

And he does it all in the city he's dreamt about since he was 10 years old.

6

The Fans Get to The Fan

Obviously, I was always a big sports guy my whole life. But when I was in a car, when I was in my previous life, I was always into music. I was listening to music all the time. But everything changed when WFAN came into being in '87. Now I had this outlet where I could listen to sports all day, and that was kind of the beginning of my love for the station. Once Mike and the Mad Dog got together, that became a must-listen every afternoon when I was coming home, and it just kind of took off from there. They would inspire me. They would say stuff that would get me aggravated, talking about the teams I root for, whether it was the Jets, the Knicks—whoever it might have been at the time. And that would inspire me to call in. But never as a caller did I ever envision myself winding up as a talk show host. I never thought it would come to that, to be very honest with you. —JOE BENIGNO

"JOE FROM SADDLE RIVER," in so many ways, represented the be-all, end-all of WFAN in the early years, the very reason the station existed to begin with. He was the quintessential New York sports fan who made the most of the forum that the all-sports launching pad gave callers on a daily basis. He never got cheated on a call; he entertained the hosts, the listeners, and himself; and when he was finished, everyone walked away from the process knowing just how much his teams meant to him. It was that unchained, undeterred love for the Jets, Mets, Knicks, and Rangers that made "Joe" a must listen. He represented the pulse of New York sports and the New York sports fan.

Somewhere along the way, the man known less for his full name—Joe Benigno—started to become more than just a caller. His opinions were so sharp, his complaints so valid, his tenor so enthusiastic. And whether or not the WFAN hosts—many times it was Mike Francesa and Chris Russo—truly respected his ability and sports knowledge in the early going is up to interpretation. Perhaps they were just playing along with him. Perhaps they just wanted to get a rise out of him, and in turn, get a few laughs from the audience. Either way, the food salesman from Bergen County, New Jersey, was starting to develop a knack for this sports radio thing. He was taking it for all it was worth.

"I was a salesman and I would go in every morning to the city. Of course, the first thing I would do was buy the papers—the *Daily News*, the *Post*, and all of that. So, I remember driving into work one day and I'm reading this column from the *New York Post's* Phil Mushnick about how FAN was going to give a caller a show. It was Eli in Westchester, who has since passed away. I'm reading this article about him getting a show and I'm saying, 'Are you kidding me? They're going to give this guy, Eli in Westchester, his own show on The Fan? You've got to be kidding me! What has this guy done except try to be controversial? Everything was racially motivated with him. Is that the only reason this guy is getting a show? Whatever,'" Benigno exclaimed. "Anyway, so that day—I'll never forget that day—when Mike and the Mad Dog came on, all they're talking about the whole day is this column by Mushnick and how there are so many other callers who deserve a show before Eli, okay? Obviously, I was thinking the same thing.

"And it turns out that they mention *me* being one of them. They mention about 10 or 12 different guys and they mentioned me, 'Joe in Saddle River.' 'He would deserve a show before Eli,' yada, yada. So, by the time I got home that day, they had already decided to have this day where they're going to bring a bunch of callers in to do a show. Not just Eli, they were going to have some other guys do it, too."

Suddenly, Benigno—of course flattered by the mere mention from Francesa and Russo—thought he might have a chance to prove his worth on the air. Not that he was planning on it before that day started, not that he dreamt of it when he loaded his Melba Foods truck that morning, but as long as the drive-time big boys on WFAN were vouching for him, hey, he had a shot, right?

"I get home and call up the show and basically try to sell myself on the air to Mike and Chris. They ask me a couple different things, I responded quickly, and finally, Francesa says, 'Look, can you give Mark Chernoff a call tomorrow? We're going to have you come in and be one of the guys.' It was tremendous."

There Benigno was, back at home in Jersey after a long day of driving around the city, and his life had changed in the blink of an eye and the length of a phone call. Joe from Saddle River had a chance, an at-bat to see if he could be more than just, well, "Joe from Saddle River."

"That's how I got the opportunity to come in on what they called Fan Appreciation Day. I was able to come in and do a show for an hour, the same day as Eli, and they also had a couple other guys come in. It was Al in White Plains and it was Vic in Corona."

Benigno was confident, bordering on cocky, after that. Did he know the ins and outs of the radio business? No. But he knew sports. And more specifically, he knew New York sports better, he thought, than those "three other guys." Not that it was a contest against the rest; it was truly a show of appreciation from WFAN, a way to give back to the callers, the listeners, and maybe generate a few laughs along the way.

"There was no pressure. I felt no pressure at all. I didn't even look at it as an opportunity for anything for the future. There was none of that. I didn't know what was going to come of it. But I went in and I did my thing. I felt very good about what I did," Benigno said.

"I'll never forget it. I did my show and I'm driving home listening to who else? Eli. They put Eli in the prime-time slot, of course. I think I was on from 3:00 to 4:00 PM, and I think Eli was on from 5:00 to 7:00 PM or whatever the hell it was. Anyhow, I remember listening to him and going, 'This guy is terrible!' All this tough talk he was doing, now when he was actually taking calls from callers, guys were basically putting his feet to the fire and he couldn't handle it! You could tell, you know what I mean? I thought that was interesting.

"The next day I remember driving my kids back up to Massachusetts to their mother because I was split up from my first wife at the time. And coming back, Francesa's on the air by himself. And his whole show, he's talking about how I was the only one of the guys who did the show the day before that had a chance to make it in the business, all right?"

Suddenly, his life changed again. Not only did he get an at-bat at WFAN, he appeared to have hit a home run. How's that for a pick-me-up on the slow, holiday-clogged commute back to New Jersey from New England?

"I'm like, 'Holy shit, you've got to be kidding me!'" Benigno said. "So I get home—obviously this was a time when there were no cell phones—in time to get on his show. I make it and get on and say, 'Thank you for all the kind words,' and it just kind of went from there."

The spark had been lit. Here was this lifelong sports fan who had a chance to see how the other half lived, to see what it'd be like to work every day as, well, a lifelong sports fan. It was truly heaven on earth. But how could he make it work long term?

"I had a lot of help from Bob Gelb, who's now a salesperson here at WFAN, and who was Mike and Chris' producer at the time. He kind of guided me into what I had to do," Benigno recalled. "I wound up going to Connecticut School of Broadcasting. I don't know how much that helped. While I was doing that, Gelb told me, 'Look, you've got to get on the air somewhere you can be heard. Even if you have go somewhere and buy time or whatever. You're going to have to do it.'

"So I found this little station in Elizabeth, New Jersey. It was called WJBM. I forget how much it cost me per show but I signed up to do 10 shows or whatever it was. It was a one-hour show on a Monday night at around 6:30 or 7:30 PM. I don't know if anybody could hear me or not, but I did a couple of those shows, and it was fun.

"I kept telling Gelb this is what I was doing, and I asked, 'Is there any way that I could have Mike and Chris come on and be guests on my show?' He said, 'Yeah, we can probably do that.' I think it was the third show I did that I had Russo on. And the next week, I had Francesa on. While I'm interviewing Mike, he's going on and talking about how Steve Somers is going to be leaving the overnight, and he said, 'They may be looking for a new overnight guy. You never know, it might be you.' I'm like, 'Yeah, come on. That's not happening.' And this is all on the air on my little, stupid, paid show. So he basically asked me, 'Could you change your lifestyle? Let's say you got the overnight gig. Could you change your lifestyle to conform to those hours?' I said, 'Of course. Absolutely.'

"About two days later, I'm calling Mike and Chris' show. I want to thank them for coming on my little stupid show. While I'm on hold, Gelb tells me, 'I don't want to make any promises but you may be hearing from Mark Chernoff about possibly filling in part time on the station.' I said 'Wow, okay.' The next day, sure enough, I get a phone call from Chernoff and he asked me to come in.'"

This is where you see the true genius of Chernoff shining through. Chernoff has always had the knack for making important, program-defining, station-altering decisions without the fear of failure...or so it appears. It's about feel for him, whether it appears like the smart call at the time or not. If it works in his eyes, it's likely going to work in New York's eyes before too long. His track record says so.

"Listen," former WFAN program director Eric Spitz said, "you're talking about a man in Mark Chernoff who has worked with Howard Stern, Don Imus, Mike Francesa, and Chris Russo. The names don't get much bigger than that in radio."

Joe Benigno wasn't about to join that guest list, at least not right away, but it didn't matter. Chernoff saw Benigno for what he was: energetic, enthusiastic, emotional, and above all else, a skilled, improving novelty who was going to make waves on the air, win, lose or draw. Benigno wasn't your typical hire, stolen away from another station in an every-man-for-himself world. He was an "Ordinary Joe," no pun intended, who gave hope to callers and fans everywhere. He was a walk-on, fresh off the practice squad, no scholarship, no pedi-gree, no nothing. He was *Hoosiers*, *Rudy*, and *Invincible* all wrapped up into one. He was simply given a microphone, an hour of airtime, and a chance to live the dream.

Before long, he was also given a job.

Only in America.

"I filled in weekends in July, and then we got into August," Benigno said. "Chernoff said to me, 'I'd like to see if you can do an entire week of the overnight. Can you get the time off from your regular job?' I said, 'Yeah, I'll take a vacation week. Absolutely.'

"So I took the vacation week and did the whole week of shows. I remember getting home that Friday morning, going to sleep, the whole thing. One of my daughters wakes me up and says, 'You've got to call Mark Chernoff. You got a call from him.'

"So I call him and Chernoff basically says to me, 'The overnight show is yours if you want it. And if you do, we're going to announce it today on *Mike and the Mad Dog*, and we'd like you to come on with them at some point.' 'Are you kidding me?' I kept asking myself. 'Are you kidding me?' I couldn't believe it. And that was it. They announced it, that started it, and it kind of took off from there. Unbelievable."

It sure was. The Fan had hired perhaps its biggest fan. It was a move that was bold, brave, and in keeping with the station's groundbreaking tradition. The Fan needed an overnight host to replace the legendary Steve Somers, who was moving to the daytime. And Benigno, Chernoff felt, fit the bill.

Those were big shoes to fill, of course, as Somers—known as "Captain Midnight" back then—had developed an overnight schtick and was followed by a family of listeners and callers cultivated through years of middle-of-the-night moments. The overnight was his domain, and he did it so well that he was bumped up to the mid-day slot with Russ Salzberg, in an attempt to boost the ratings in between *Imus in the Morning* and *Mike and the Mad Dog*.

"I was never worried about the overnight," Somers said. "Would I miss it—the time, the callers, the whole bit? Sure. But Joe was a must-listen, especially when he was ranting about the Jets. His rants, to me, were to die for, and you had to listen. I knew he'd be just fine."

Somers wasn't alone.

Benigno did a few things right from the start that were integral to his short-term success. First, he built his own brand and made it clear that his show wasn't going to be Steve Somers version 2.0. He appreciated, respected, and admired Somers and his significant success, of course. But Benigno knew he landed this dream position by being himself; he made it to the mic by being Joe from Saddle River. There was no reason to change now. What you heard, as a result, was a fan's fan in every way, ranting about the losses and raving about the wins at the top of his lungs. Jets, Mets, Knicks, Rangers—it didn't matter. The same passion and pride was there, the delivery was just a little different. Now he was on the mic, not on the telephone.

Second, as a famous caller himself, he knew what it was like to be on other side of that WFAN line, and he created an unbreakable bond with his listeners, and more specifically with those who picked up the telephone and helped his show. Those were Joe's people: the callers.

"And you still hear that every day," said Spitz. "There is such a strong relationship there, an appreciation between Joe and his callers. And he always ends his show by thanking them."

"Want to thank the callers. Great job as always. Could not do it without you."

That is Benigno's signoff every day. Too often callers at any radio station can sometimes feel left out, forgotten, used as nothing more than time fillers until the next celebrity guest comes on or the next sports update is cued. Benigno never traveled down that road.

"I never had any problem getting calls," he said. "And I always felt the overnight show was never about me, it was always about the callers. It's definitely a caller-driven show—a lot of crazy personalities, a lot of people who made the show what it was. I knew once I got through my opening, whatever my opening was, that the rest of it was going to be gravy because of the callers."

And it didn't take long for the powers-that-be to notice.

"Like Steve with his overnight, Joe treated the callers as if they were family, and they would be allowed to stay on the air a little longer and address several things," Spitz said. "And that's what the overnight is. Joe was great with that."

It's important to have a solid support staff as well, especially in the overnight. It can break things up, it can help the host segue into other topics, and it can allow the listeners to hear another voice for a change of pace. One of Benigno's key cogs was an upstart update man named Don La Greca.

La Greca was a perfect yin for Benigno's yang because in the late 1990s, as Benigno's star began to rise, hockey was a huge focus in New York. Between the Rangers and the Devils, the area won the Stanley Cup in 1994 and 1995, and that carried over to some tremendous playoff series including—and between—those two franchises.

This was perfect for the overnight, because Benigno was a die-hard Rangers fan and La Greca was a die-hard Devils fan. As a result, the latter would come on the air and give the Devils' side of things, becoming something of a New Jersey beat reporter, and the two could toss around several other hockey items.

La Greca, like Benigno, was a sports fan, first and foremost. A native of Hawthorne, New Jersey, he grew up reading the same papers and following the same stories and sports that Benigno did. The two shared an instant chemistry. La Greca was also living the dream. He cut his teeth in the business at a pre-Internet outfit called Sports Phone, where callers would receive news and score updates from journalists. La Greca cultivated his craft there, and eventually landed a spot with Benigno.

"The thing with Don was, I knew he knew sports," Benigno said. "I talk about guys in this business who really don't know that much about sports. They get by for whatever reason. I'm not going to name names, but there are guys out there who are very limited in what they know. Don wasn't like that. I always felt La Greca was a guy who knew sports inside and out."

And what a rush it was for La Greca. There was a Jersey guy getting his opportunity and making the most of it. And there was Benigno, another Jersey guy, turning La Greca's efforts into a valued piece of his show. La Greca has since taken his talent to the next level as an afternoon host on ESPN Radio 98.7 FM, WFAN's chief competition in New York. He is also a play-by-play man and rinkside analyst on the Rangers Radio Network.

"Whenever the Devils were in the playoffs, Joe would ask me to call in and talk about the game," La Greca said. "He wouldn't go on the air until 1:00 in the morning. So I'd go to the game or watch the game—this was around the period of time when the Devils couldn't make it out of the first round—and he'd always say they're overrated, the most overrated team in New York. He'd always make fun of me when I'd call in, but it was good radio.

"The thing is I was still living at home at the time and this was before cell phones. So, I'd drive around North Jersey at 2:00 in the morning waiting for him to say, 'We're waiting for La Greca to call,' and then I'd pull over to a pay phone and I'd call him up.

"We would do a whole segment talking about the Devils and what their problems were, and I just became a regular contributor to the show to talk about the team. He didn't treat me like just any other caller. That raised my profile. I'm not just somebody that barked out scores for him. He didn't have the ego: 'I have to talk to a player' or 'I have to talk to the play-by-play guy or somebody who writes for the team.' He felt me coming on to talk about the Devils and their problems was just as good as anybody who covered the team."

Eventually, Benigno—like Somers before him—grew too big for the overnight. As great a gig as it may be, there comes a point in a personality's career where the executives may decide he is better suited for a larger audience. That time came in 2004 for the man then known as Joe B. And with yet another shakeup in the midday, he was given the opportunity to move up after nine years of talking sports in the middle of the night.

At the time, Jody McDonald was the midday cohost with Sid Rosenberg. But all things end at WFAN, and that show was no different. McDonald and the station parted ways in 2004—he has since returned without missing a beat—and suddenly, Rosenberg needed a cohost. Enter Benigno, who was thrust into a new world. The time of day changed, the topics at hand changed, and the format changed. He was now working with another host, and one who often found trouble in and out of the workplace.

The Sid-Joe parlay wasn't a consistent winner. It wasn't bad radio by any means; the show featured two local guys who knew their teams, knew their callers, and knew their place in the world. It just wasn't destined to last forever.

"I thought we had a very good show together. I really did. I look at it this way: any show where I'm the straight man has to be pretty good," Benigno said, referring to Rosenberg's chemical addiction problems. "I don't know what to say. It's a shame that it didn't work out, but I always got along great with Sid. In fact, I still get along with him. We're still very good friends. I go on his show down in Florida a lot, anytime he needs me. I always enjoyed working with Sid.

"I don't look at myself as any kind of prima donna or anything like that. Like I said, there are many guys in this business who take it much too seriously and think that they're a bigger deal than they are. And I never thought of myself in that way. So I never had a problem transitioning to dealing with a partner."

That was evident in 2007, after two years of doing middays solo. Benigno held his own in the post-Rosenberg era—being alone on the air was not new to him—but the station had been looking for a replacement for Sid, and there were several up-and-comers who had earned a chance in that chair.

One candidate was Kevin Burkhardt, a fresh face who made the most of some overnight shifts and some stints as an update man. He bonded with Russo, and had received the all-important Mad Dog seal of approval, not unlike former WFAN host Ian Eagle before him. Burkhardt was another in a long line of young pros waiting for his shot on the grand stage. It seemed like just a matter of time.

"I always liked TV more, but radio just became my natural path in school. It became my first love," said Burkhardt, who moved onto television after making the difficult decision to walk away from WFAN and is now the field reporter for the New York Mets on SportsNet New York and an NFL play-by-play man for Fox. "At that time, when I was trying to rise through the station a little bit, it was the same time—for the most part—as Evan Roberts, even though he was a little bit ahead of me in terms of what he had done."

Evan Roberts was something of a WFAN prodigy. He gave updates on *Imus in the Morning* as a nine-year-old and is a genuine New York sports nut who seemed destined to have a spot on the station someday. That day finally came in January 2007, when the kid who wowed Imus years earlier got the call to sit alongside Benigno in the midday. One superfan met another.

"We had actually done a couple shows together and I knew they liked him, and rightfully so," Burkhardt said. "I think he's great. For me, the timing worked out great. I could see that Evan was going to get a chance at the next big opportunity, which obviously came up. That place, those opportunities, don't come often. I enjoyed the hell out of my time there and I learned so much and did so many great things, but in the terms of career advancement, SNY came, and it was just perfect timing for me."

It was perfect for Roberts, too. While Benigno, who turned 60 in September of 2013, gave hope to longtime dreamers who wanted a shot at greatness, Roberts, who was 24 when he snared the midday gig, gave hope to the *younger* dreamers. He represented a new generation of New York sports fan, a guy who clicked with Benigno because of their shared allegiance to the Mets and Jets. They differed in basketball and hockey—Roberts sides with the Nets and the Islanders—but that added to the show, as well.

Roberts, as young as he was, understood the guiding principle of the station: that the callers made the shows work. It helped that he started as a fill-in overnight host. Like Somers and Benigno before him, Roberts became one with that family of callers, the loyal, lost souls awake in the middle of the night. And when you add it all up, it was another wise move by Chernoff and Co. The transition was seamless.

"I was very naïve. I never thought I was in any competition for that job, to be honest with you," Roberts said. "It was two overnights a week, Monday morning and Friday morning, which is great during the football season, and I was working my regular, full-time job at Sirius," said Roberts, who began to make a name for himself in satellite radio. "So I had two gigs at the same time and I was kind of happy. I didn't think about moving up or anything. The few times that I filled in with Joe, when they moved me up, it was a great experience. Maybe it was because I was naïve, but I just didn't think, *Oh, it would be cool to do middays with Joe.* I was like, 'Hey, I'm doing overnights. This is great. I'll probably do this for the next 10 years. And it'll be great.'

"Luckily, Joe and I had a very good relationship from the beginning. I give him a ton of credit, because when we filled in for the first time for *Mike and the Mad Dog*, he could have said, 'Who the hell is this young punk? Who's this schmuck?' But luckily, right away, he was introducing me to everybody. 'This is Ev. Young guy, likes the Mets.' That made it a lot easier, and I think the fact that we had the same favorite football and baseball team was a big help.

"When they called me up and said 'We're offering you midday,' I was stunned! I thought I was going to get full-time overnights or something. I had no idea. So I was in heaven! By the time we started working together I had already done shows with him, and we already had a good relationship. So it was a very easy transition because of him."

That relationship continues today. Roberts and Benigno have spent the better part of six years together and have an eclectic mix of regular guests and loyal callers. They have also taken advantage of some roller-coaster years from the Jets to fuel many a show. The Jets have played in two AFC Championship Games since the two joined together and have also been a fixture in the tabloids. It's resulted in an answer, a resolution to the midday malaise that has plagued the station for decades.

"I don't think we have any strategy other than being ourselves. One thing about Joe and me, we're the same guys off the air. The arguments and discussions we have off the air are the exact same things you hear on the air—which is why I don't like talking to Joe that much about sports off the air, because we want to save it. We want it to be completely natural," Roberts said. "We're very passionate fans and come from different angles. He's the old, grizzled veteran and I'm a young guy.

"When we do fight and yell—there's this [former Mets outfielder] Carlos Beltran argument that people tell me they like listening to, where we yelled and screamed—it's all in good fun. I went back and listened to the Beltran thing, and I don't think we were ever going to kill each other, but I think we were passionate about it. That's just us.

"We agree a lot. What are you going to do? We're never just going to force a disagreement because people can see right through it. So when we do have a disagreement, I think it's good radio because it's 100 percent natural."

It doesn't go unnoticed, either.

"When you look at someone like Evan Roberts, it's amazing," Spitz said. "Here you have someone who has grown into a proven radio professional and he's barely 30 years old."

Benigno concurred with Spitz's assessment.

"I think he's unbelievable. Most guys his age think if it happened before 1990, it didn't happen," Benigno said. "You're not going to find a lot of guys who know what's going on in sports like he does, but also know the history of it all, who are barely 30 years old. He knows the history of sports as good as anybody who's lived it for the most part.

"I think that's the thing with our show in general. I don't think there's any sports show out there that has two guys who know as much as we do."

Benigno set the table for the likes of Roberts, the hosts who are fans first, radio stars second. In an era of former athletes and print journalists grabbing talk shows of their own, it is not lost on the WFAN listeners that these guys are just like them. Familiarity breeds contentment.

"Joe is a remarkable story. Since I was a kid, I wanted to be on the radio. It's all I wanted. I think what's incredible about him is in the middle of his life, he had a career change and learned not just how to be on the radio, but how to do all the little things that listeners don't realize," Roberts said. "He's definitely a tremendous host. I think of my dad, being a CPA, and all of a sudden, one day he just says, 'I don't want to be a CPA anymore. I want to be a talk show host.' It'd be quite a transition for him, and that's what Joe did. He's been able to pull it off. Definitely, definitely cool."

That's an interesting way to describe it: cool. Benigno—remember, we said he is a confident sort—sees it the same way.

"All I'll say is this: I'm going to be 60 years old [in 2013], which is stunning to me. That I'm actually going to be 60…that's a very scary number. Although there are very few people my age who are as *cool* as I am. I'll be the first to say that. Tough to dispute that. If you know me, I'm as cool a 60-year-old as one can possibly be.

"With that said, I'm still 60 and I would not want to be a relic who's hanging on. I don't want to be a guy who has lost his fastball and is still doing this. I don't know when that time will come. If all things go well—unless somebody's paying me just stupid money to do this, outrageous money—at 65, I could see myself walking away, to be very honest. Whether that happens or not, I don't know.

"But that's the only thing I'll say. I cannot see me being some guy that doesn't really have it anymore, just going out there, still doing my thing. I don't want to be that. I want to get out while I've still got it."

Which is the exact same way "Joe from Saddle River" got in.

7

Here's Mink with the 20/20

I would never be able to do what they do, or want to do it. One time, I did an update and I just decided to say the five things that were going on in sports and throw it to a commercial. It was awful. It's difficult, especially when there are games going on, because you don't want to be behind the Internet and everyone's phone is giving them instant updates. To sit there and write and rewrite and rewrite...I have no idea what the order of news should be, but I always know that they do. And of course, it all starts with Mink. He is a legend. I hear John Minko's voice, it's like, boom, *WFAN. His name and his voice are synonymous with the station. That's a pretty cool thing.*
—EVAN ROBERTS

JOHN MINKO STOOD AT CENTER COURT IN PHILADELPHIA, sporting his patented perma-smile from ear to ear with his right hand on his chin, simply trying to soak in the moment. The radio play-by-play man for St. John's basketball, Minko had just called a buzzer beater that lifted the Red Storm into the second round of the NIT on March 19, 2013, and you can excuse him if he was a bit satisfied. St. John's, after all, was moving on to another postseason game, which meant more work for him, and when it came time to broadcast the winning shot against St. Joseph's to the masses, well, he nailed it.

"Give us the call again, Mink!"

"Tell it to us like you told it to them, John!"

"Yeah, you can do it for us, Mink!"

Minko obliged, of course. He was surrounded by St. John's personnel who were also ecstatic after Red Storm sophomore guard Sir'Dominic Pointer blew by press row and connected on a last-second jumper that gave St. John's a 63–61 victory over a stunned St. Joseph's team on Hawk Hill. It wasn't an NCAA tournament win, certainly. And the Red Storm only survived to play one more round before their season ended against Virginia in a 68–50 loss that wasn't even *that* close. So, this win over the Hawks was hardly the stuff of legends. But it was a proud moment on the road for a rebuilding program, and the parties involved wanted to relive it.

Say no more when it comes to the Mink Man. He looked down, tapped his left foot twice, collected his thoughts, and with the body language of a radio professional some 30 years in the making, he delivered the winning shot once again in front of a three-man standing audience.

"Yeah," he said humbly afterward, "Why not, right? Give them what they want."

It shouldn't be a surprise, of course. That's exactly what he's been doing with WFAN listeners for nearly 27 years.

The godfather of the station's patented 20/20 sports updates, Minko is the fun-loving, playful guy in the corner who always seems to be there when you need him. He gets the best gigs—working on

Mike Francesa's shows primarily—he gets plenty of airtime, and he is one of the original members of the station.

You can forget about him sometimes, of course. Let's face it, in the course of WFAN's 24-hour broadcasting day, Minko's 2:40 PM update on the Yankees bullpen or Rangers captain Ryan Callahan's hamstring may not stand out. But when news is being made, you can always count on him to deliver the goods. He does it eloquently, efficiently, and energetically.

And he has forged a path for the legion of update anchors, near and far, to follow.

"I don't think about it that way," he said with a laugh and a nod. "I've just been here a long time, and they had to find something for me to do."

It wasn't always that way for Minko, who has sat in a chair only a select few ever have in the life of this station. In fact, after Greg Gumbel's ill-fated attempt at a morning show in the early days of WFAN, and before Don Imus made the move to the station and changed things forever, this little guy from Bergenfield, New Jersey, was in that slot.

In 1988, WFAN launched the *Minko Morning Zoo*, and as you were driving into the city amid the morning rush at the George Washington Bridge or Lincoln Tunnel, you heard Minko try to deliver the wit and wisdom expected from a high-profile show.

It didn't work out.

"No, it did not. Definitely not," he said with a laugh. "You learn a lot in this business, and we were learning a lot about the station back then. I learned, too. I learned that I'm not a talk show host, and that I'll never be a talk show host. I think, looking back on it, I was a talk show host for about three weeks there—in between Greg and Imus—so, if nothing else, I'm the answer to a trivia question. 'Who bridged that gap of three weeks?' That was me.

"I did sportscasts when I was in Indianapolis before coming here 26 years ago, and basically, that's what I do. I know my role."

In a business in which so many people don't, it is refreshing to encounter people who do. Minko is not alone, of course; WFAN's stable of longtime updaters continue to entertain and inform. Many have passed through the station's doors and moved on to other ventures, but many have stayed because they love what they do. While the face of sports news in the era of mobile devices has changed, many of the faces who deliver the updates—including Minko's, Rich Ackerman's, and Bob Huessler's—have not.

"We do kind of raise people," WFAN operations manager Mark Chernoff said. "When I came to WFAN to 1993, about a month after I got here, I decided to do the 20/20s, and I got it from WOR FM, a station from long ago, that eventually became 99X, and then KISS, and 98.7. Anyway, they used to do 20/20 news, and I had this idea in my head to do 20/20 sports, and we did them to see if it worked.

"When I first started looking for people for those spots, I was looking for people to do both anchor and host. Ian Eagle could do both. Steve Levy could do both. But some people were just cut out for the updates. They love the sportscasts, they know how to condense the stuff into a minute or two minutes, and how to get that information out with the right pacing. And that's what they want to do. And that's what we need them to do, so it works.

"They don't always want to get on the air and have an opinion about something every single day, where you have to know all of the Xs and Os, and perform all the monologues, and talk to the callers every day. Some people don't want that.

"So, I started to realize that not everyone is going to do both. Now, I look for hosts when I need a host and anchors when I need an anchor. We have had some who can still do both since then—Bob Wischusen was one, Chris Carlin was one, Marc Malusis, too—but

Two WFAN origi-
nals: Jim Lampley
(top), who went on
to a long career at
HBO Sports, and
Jody McDonald,
whose years at the
station included a
run as the midday
host. *(HBO/WIP 94
FM)*

The addition of Don Imus to The Fan's lineup in 1988 marked a turning point for the station. *(Getty Images)*

Sid Rosenberg made a name for himself as the sports update man on *Imus in the Morning.* He proved to be one of the more outspoken and controversial voices in the station's history. *(640 AM Sports Florida)*

Dave Sims was a trailblazer in sports radio, hosting the *SportsNight* show on WNBC before joining The Fan in the early 1990s. *(Seattle Mariners)*

Arguably the greatest sports radio show of all time, *Mike and the Mad Dog*, hosted by Mike Francesa (left) and Chris Russo, set the standard by which all other shows are measured.

A former producer on *Mike and the Mad Dog*, Marc Malusis jumped into an overnight role and also hosts on the CBS Sports Radio Network. *(SportsNet New York)*

When the station went looking for someone to take over the morning show in the wake of Don Imus' departure, management selected the duo of Boomer Esiason (left) and Craig Carton. *(WFAN)*

Evan Roberts (left), shown here in The Fan's old studio before the station moved to its current location in the CBS Radio facility. *(WFAN)*

Legend of the overnight shift Steve Somers (left) and listener turned host Joe Benigno are two of the more passionate hosts on The Fan. *(WFAN)*

Many WFAN alums have gone on to national broadcasting careers, including Steve Levy (top) and Ian Eagle (bottom, right). *(ESPN/YES Network)*

Kenny Albert (top, right) began his career at WFAN as a teen-ager; today he is the only play-by-play man broadcasting all four major professional sports. *(MSG Network)*

Kevin Burkhardt served as over-night host on The Fan in the early 2000s. He now covers the Mets for SportsNet New York. *(SportsNet New York)*

Sweeny Murti, shown here throwing a baseball back to Derek Jeter, is The Fan's Yankees beat reporter. *(Sweeny Murti)*

Chris Carlin filled a variety of roles during his years at The Fan and now hosts SNY's Mets pregame and postgame shows. *(SportsNet New York)*

we really try to find what niche works best when we're trying to find a role for someone."

As far as Minko is concerned, his role is to deliver the news.

"First of all, other than my family, WFAN is my professional life. It's 26 years and we're hopefully going to keep going. It's what we do, and the impact of the radio station in my professional life, it is the top," Minko said. "And over the course of the station, yes, many people have been update people, you do get close to them, and we're all after the same thing: to bring the news to you, the important stories, and to do it quickly.

"We've developed into a very close group, all of us, and I'm not just talking about the people who are on the air. I'm talking about the producers. I'm talking about everybody. People in the sales department, traffic, everybody. We all have jobs to do to make the station great.

"It's got to be that way."

And that has its rewards. Without question, over the years WFAN's hosts have become celebrities in New York and beyond, but the update men have gotten in the mix, too. When you are broadcast on MSG Network, like morning update anchor Jerry Recco is on *Boomer & Carton*, or the YES Network, like Minko, Ackerman, and Huessler are on *Mike's On*, Francesa's afternoon drive-time show, people are going to remember you.

But it goes beyond the standard exposure that cable television brings. The hosts—and in particular, the current talent, including Boomer Esiason, Craig Carton, Joe Benigno, Steve Somers, Roberts, and Francesa—often open the microphone to allow the updaters a chance to speak their mind. Maybe it was what they did last weekend. Maybe it was their take on the Mets' batting order. Maybe it was a little back and forth on the end of that St. John's thriller of a game in Philadelphia. No matter the instance, these guys usually take full advantage, and listeners remember that.

"Television, sure, it's changed my life. I get recognized on the street. I get recognized on the train. I get recognized in the ShopRite in my town. That's exciting, but it's more about the feedback they give you and what you give them," Minko said. "My philosophy has always been, if I walk outside the station and make a left, and you're coming toward me on the street and say 'Well, how ya doing, Mink?' I'll say 'I'm doing fine.' Then you may ask me, 'What's going on in the world of sports?' And for like 45 seconds, I'll tell you what's going on like I was on the air. Can't help it.

"Like I said, give them what they want."

Ackerman does the same, but like most everyone at The Fan, he does it in his own way.

A New Yorker who fine-tuned his radio career in Chicago, Ackerman—perhaps more than most at the station—truly appreciates the privilege of doing what he does in the city that he does it in. He is an update man—not a host, not an icon. But he still lives the dream and strives every day to appreciate it.

"The power of the station and the allure of the station was somewhat always there, but I never really felt that need or urgency to be there. I really enjoyed my time elsewhere—I lived very briefly in Charlotte and I was in Washington for nearly two years and really loved Washington," Ackerman said. "I was able to get the *New York Post* every day or the *New York Times*, and I never really felt like 'Boy, I've got to get back to New York again' at that point. I thought of it as having the best of all worlds.

"But then I went to Chicago, and things changed. I thought Chicago would have been a place I would have enjoyed living, and it just did not work out. It was very provincial. So that was the first place where I kind of felt 'You know what, this really isn't for me, and I have a home and it's not here. It's back in New York.' So that was the impetus for me try to get back here, and it kind of also came at a point in my personal life when my friends were starting to have kids and other friends were starting to get married. I was in my mid-to-late twenties at that point, and I saw everybody else moving on and I was going to be in a spot where I was isolated from everybody. My friends are very important to me. My family, too. And I just saw everybody going in a different direction—and I don't want to say I was shut out—but I was unable to be part of things."

It made sense, of course. Ackerman graduated from NYU and was a roommate of play-by-play broadcaster Kenny Albert there. So you can imagine the sports discussions that went on in that room. In fact, sports were about all there was for those two back then. Ackerman used to grab a *New York Post* before class in the mornings and read it at his desk, hidden behind a textbook. It's that kind of passion, that sort of city pride, that eventually got the man they call "Ack" back to New York.

"When Kenny got engaged, I was in Chicago, and everybody was there in New York. It just happened to coincide with a barbeque party that he was having the next day. And everybody was there to celebrate but me. I kind of felt left out. So at that point I decided that I wanted to come back here," said Ackerman.

"I watched the '96 Final Four at Kenny's apartment—I just happened to be in town at that point—and I remember driving from Times Square at midnight. I remember seeing the whole thing lit up. Growing up as a kid, the city, the rush of the city, was very impressive to me. But all of a sudden, all of the lights just kind of lit up, and I was like 'Wow, this is it. This is New York.' It just came together at that moment. I knew I needed to be a part of that."

That chance came at WFAN, and as had happened to so many others at the station, the door opened for Ackerman thanks to contacts made earlier in life. Albert, in fact, had developed a strong relationship with Eric Spitz, the program director at WFAN, and eventually Ack was set up with a gig that he still cherishes to this day.

And along the way, he has developed into a bit of a celebrity.

You see, Ackerman can have conversations with anyone. He is a professional talker, and that appeals to a great many in New York. One such person is former television-morning-show host Regis Philbin. Members at the same gym, Philbin and Ackerman developed a friendship and Philbin—a loyal listener—got to talking one day about Ackerman's love life.

A familiar topic on *Mike and the Mad Dog* back in the day, Ackerman's dating resume could have used an upgrade and so Philbin thought he'd chip in. He set up what was called "Project Ack Ack," in which Rich would go on *Live with Regis and Kelly* and participate in a reality-show-type contest in which he found the perfect date.

"I was on quite a bit. We did filming one day, but then it was cut up into four different episodes. I was on for over a month," he said with a laugh. "I did the first thing where they got to know me. Then they set me up with a guy who was supposed to be a coach, so to speak. Give me an edge because they thought I was too nice. So I did that. And then we did the whole meet the girls, which they split up into four things...and then the date itself. It was an experience."

Suddenly, Ack, an unassuming, aw-shucks guy from Brooklyn, was a star. And not just in New York.

Everywhere.

"I was on national television seven or eight times. I also did a whole makeover episode. That was something. It was more than I ever imagined and more fun than I ever imagined. It stretched over a month. I became very close with the staff during the process. At first it was a whirlwind. It happened and a couple days later, there they are shooting your life story, and then you're on. 'My God, look at how this is unfurling!'

"Then you kind of get your feet under you. You know how to plan. All of a sudden, I was this guy in demand. I've got Regis trying to get me a date! You get swept up in all of it."

So, too, did Rachel, the winner of the contest. The two went to a Rangers game—the cameras went along, of course—and "Project Ack Ack" came to a close.

"We talked a little afterward, but it was really all that one date. I actually wound up dating another girl who was one of the girls on the show. We dated for several months after that. But that kind of ran its course. But it was all fun. How can you hate the attention?

"There were hundreds of girls from the inquiries, yes. But it really hit me when I showed up at the Empire Hotel that night for the filming and here are 14 girls that are coming from Pittsburgh, Vancouver, Houston, and here in town…to see me! You're like 'Wow, this is pretty impressive. They're all here to meet me? Are you sure about this?' It was overwhelming and it was also very flattering."

Not bad for a WFAN update man, right?

"And then all of a sudden it ends so abruptly. You see it coming. You get used to it. It took me a week or so to get used to it and then you really soak it all in. Then you see the end. Not that I'm a person who needs my ego stroked or anything like that, but it's quite a comedown. You've been living the life for a month and all of a sudden, *boom*, it's all over.

"Back to the station."

And back to the 20/20s.

"It's a role that needs to be filled and you get used to it," said Ackerman, who now primarily does updates on the CBS Sports Radio Network. "I think the important thing is to know what you have going, know yourself, know what the format is, and just go. You have to be able to pace yourself. You have to know what's going on and where, and how you can handle yourself throughout the day. I think once you get that experience, you ultimately find a rhythm.

"I always liked being self-deprecating. I understand that this is a team here at WFAN, and I'm a guy just looking to be in the clubhouse and not rock the boat. You accept the role, and for me I'm very good at playing the foil, so I'll do that."

For some, opportunity knocks elsewhere—even somewhere else not as proven as WFAN. Perhaps it's a bigger role at a smaller station. Perhaps it's a different role at a newer station. Either way, many hit that fork in the road and choose to walk away from the station they grew up listening to.

"It was hard. It was my dream job. It was *the* station," said Don La Greca, a former update man at WFAN who has moved on to a talk show career at ESPN FM 98.7, The Fan's chief rival. "But you come to that crossroads in your career where you say to yourself, 'If I stay here, I'm pigeonholed into just being the update guy, the anchor, the part-time host.' I needed to go someplace where I could do what I wanted to do.

"I use the analogy that I was playing for the New York Yankees, but I was riding the bench. I decided I'd go play for the Pittsburgh Pirates, where I had a chance to start. As much as I loved WFAN, at that particular time, the opportunities at The Fan just weren't there for me to spread my wings and do what I wanted to do. Not that going to ESPN is going to any small-time thing, because it's ESPN. But at the same time it was a start-up radio station in New York. So you knew you were starting from ground zero.

"But I felt I had to take that chance if I was really going to do what I wanted to do. I could have stayed at the place that I loved so much, but if I really wasn't doing what I wanted to do, was it worth it? So it was tough but it was something I knew I had to do. There was never a point in time where I regretted it or felt like it was something I couldn't do, because my career and doing what I wanted to do was more important than being where I wanted to be.

"Looking back at it, it was the right decision to make."

Others have made the same call, with varied results. Steve Levy, long before La Greca took the microphone at WFAN, was an update man while he was plotting out a career that also landed him at ESPN.

Different circumstances, of course. La Greca left to be a competitive radio host in New York. Levy left to be a play-by-play guy and anchorman for the "Worldwide Leader in Sports."

One can't fault either individual, of course. But no matter where they go, no matter what games they call, no matter what sites they broadcast from, people still remember their days as update guys. It remains a badge of honor.

"I'll never forget those days, that's for sure. And I still get it everywhere I go," Levy said. "It's amazing for the radio station because I wasn't there long, and people continue to remember and recognize what I did there. Truly amazing."

Levy was an update anchor for a Saturday morning show with Richard Neer. The popular weekend 10:00 AM–to–1:00 PM shift was a show that eventually landed in Chris Russo's hands, and now Roberts does it.

"They remember hearing me on those updates. I was on with Richard Neer, a popular show, and people listened. They were out and about doing things, running errands, what have you, and they had The Fan on," Levy said.

"Believe me, for every time someone comes up to me and says 'You're the *SportsCenter* guy,' there's someone else who says 'Hey, I used to listen to you on WFAN all those years ago.' I'm always amazed by that. And I'm not just talking about getting that in New

York. I get it everywhere. You're talking about a station that is now a power not just locally but nationally."

La Greca, as well, will never forget some of his updates, and some of the people who helped him reach that point.

"Training with John Minko, that was special," he said. "You grow up listening to the station, you know these guys so well for what they do on the air, and then all of a sudden, there I was, training with them. It was a tremendous experience."

La Greca is not alone. The list of people Minko has trained through the years is a long one. And he's never shied away from sharing what he's learned. That's just Mink being Mink.

"I'm just trying to do the best I can. The one thing that is difficult about that is, I can teach them, but if I teach them to do it exactly how I do it, that's not a good idea," Minko said. "So sometimes teaching can be difficult because everybody's got their own style. What you want to do is teach them what they need to know and let them figure out how to go about getting it out there. So, sometimes it's a little difficult, but I try to do the best I can, and hope that it works out for everybody. But in the end, it's up to them, and they usually run with that.

"That's why we all have different names and different styles. That's what makes WFAN what it is, and that's what makes the 20/20s what they are, I suppose."

Give them what they want, Mink.

8

Meet the Mets, Meet the Mets

I remember talking about it with friends of mine in the upper deck of Shea Stadium when we were kids. 'Wouldn't it be great if there was a station that just played old games?' That's really how I envisioned an all-sports station. Not so much in terms of telephone talk, but wouldn't it be great if there was a station that was just playing all kinds of old games? As talk radio became more successful and there were sports talk shows, it was still kind of a daunting thought that there would be a station doing it 24/7. I was very—I wouldn't say skeptical—but cynical, anyway, about the chances it could thrive. There's a difference between surviving and thriving. But there was always the Mets. And I thought, The Mets are hot and the station's kind of built around them. For now, while the Mets are good, the station can be reasonably successful.

—HOWIE ROSE

THE YEAR WAS 1986. *Crocodile Dundee* and *Ferris Bueller's Day Off* were among the nation's top-grossing movies. "That's What Friends Are For," a collaboration by music legends Dionne Warwick, Elton John, Stevie Wonder and Gladys Knight, was the top song in America. Halley's Comet made it to its perihelion, the closest point to the sun.

And in New York sports, a ragtag baseball team in Queens was the toast of the town. To steal a title from another film of that year, the Amazin' Mets were New York's "Top Gun."

They were stars. They were slick. They were skilled.

And they knew it.

With manager Davey Johnson leading the way, the confident Mets strolled to a 108–54 record with barely a hiccup in 1986. A deep lineup scored 783 runs en route to a National League East title, as the fans turned out en masse—the team drew 2,767,601 of them in the regular season alone—to see the brash, bustling bunch.

The playoffs were no cakewalk, of course. New York outlasted the Houston Astros in six suspenseful games to win the National League, and then the team combined with Boston to redefine the word *drama* in a World Series no true sports fan who lived through it will ever forget. A seven-game, gut-wrenching series win over the Red Sox sealed this team's fate and placed it in the New York sports pantheon forever.

"Heeeeee struck him out! Struck...him...out! The Mets have won the World Series! And they're jamming and crowding all over Jessie Orosco! The dream has come true. The Mets have won the World Series!"

That was one of many memorable radio calls in a memorable series by Bob Murphy, the longtime play-by-play man who was with the Mets from Day 1, in their inaugural season of 1962, all the way to his retirement in 2003. Murphy died on August 3, 2004, at the age of 79.

Murphy lived through many of the ups and downs of the enigmatic franchise, and clearly the mid-1980s was among the ups. When Orosco, the team's left-handed closer, struck out Boston second baseman Marty Barrett to end the World Series, the Mets had earned just their second title in team history, and New York, as a baseball town, had its first since 1978.

It was a long time coming and it ushered in a great period for New York sports in general. The NFL's Giants were well on their way to their own dominant season, and went 14–2 in 1986. A skilled group of veterans, the Giants were led by coach Bill Parcells, quarterback Phil Simms, and linebacker Lawrence Taylor. Combined with a stout supporting cast, the Giants followed the Amazins' lead, took the city on another joyride, and won the Super Bowl on January 25, 1987, 39–20 against the Denver Broncos, in Pasadena, California.

Of course, there was no WFAN around for either of those championships. When Orosco threw up his glove and fell to his knees on that crisp autumn night, the radio station was still a twinkle in the eye of Jeff Smulyan, the CEO of Emmis Communications, an Indianapolis-based radio enterprise.

But what the Mets—and to a lesser extent, the Giants—did was create a sports buzz that fueled Smulyan's vision and the thought that all-sports could work in a place like New York, with the right staff, the right signal, and the right support.

Well, the Mets were the perfect support.

"We inherited a great team," Smulyan said. "That was key."

"Huge," former WFAN program director Eric Spitz said. "Absolutely huge. I think it's safe to say—in fact, I know it is—that the station wouldn't be where it is today without having the Mets."

Smulyan knew it, too. He knew that WHN AM 1050 was the flagship station of the Mets, and that when he purchased that country music station for $10 million he was acquiring an anchor, a foundation upon which he could build this station with a format that had so many scratching their heads. But Smulyan, who would later go on to own the Seattle Mariners, didn't need to be a full-time New Yorker to realize the power of baseball in the city and the draw that these Mets were at this time. It was the perfect fit. Start with the Mets and reap the rewards of a team that played 162 games—at the minimum—on your all-sports air.

But Smulyan and his team of executives were smart enough to think beyond the games as well. They knew a good thing when they saw it, and one of those things was expanded coverage of the Mets before and after the games, a concept formulated at WHN. It seemed so simple, of course. But sometimes, simple works.

"After the Mets had the big season that they had in '86, as they got closer to the end of the season, WHN was looking to make any extra revenue that they could from the Mets," said Howie Rose, a former sportscaster on WHN's morning show from 1977 to 1983 who moved on to WCBS AM 880 and the NBC Radio Network after his position was eliminated. "So what they did was create this pre- and postgame show for the postseason called *Mets Extra*, which was hosted by a guy named Dave Cohen, who didn't really have any recognition factor in New York. He was the host and he worked with Rusty Staub, his cohost, just for the playoffs.

"It was supposed to be a one-and-done thing. Well, obviously, it produced a lot of revenue for the station, and after the World Series, the station decided—and I only got wind of this through back channels—that they wanted to make it a full-time thing. So when the word got out that this was something they would be looking to fill, I said, 'There couldn't be a more perfect vehicle for me.' I got back in touch with the people at WHN, none of whom, other than a couple of the disc jockeys and people on the air, had been there when I left. All the management people had changed. I let them know of my interest, they brought me in, and I put together a proposal."

It should be noted that Rose, who would later go on to replace Murphy in the Mets' broadcast booth, was from Brooklyn, went to Queens College, and was every ounce a New Yorker as well as a Mets fan. He had spent his childhood in Shea's upper deck.

In short, this was his dream job.

"We clicked right away and they gave me the job. They had me back at WHN as the sports director, which meant I did the sports reports in the morning and then hosted *Mets Extra*," he said. "While I was being interviewed, there were some hints dropped that the station might become an all-sports station, which was a brand-new concept. I wasn't sure exactly what to think, but I remember on the night of my wedding, April 26, 1987, the general manager of the station, a great guy named Rick Dames, called. He called to say, 'I just want to let you know that we are going all sports, and you're going to be the seven-to-midnight guy.'

"I was probably the first guy other than the people involved at the ownership level who knew that. So that's a pretty nice wedding gift, to know that I was not only going to stay on the station doing *Mets Extra* but also have my own talk show. That was a good weekend. And that was really the turning point in my career."

And it can be traced back to this headline-making, revenue-generating, live-life-to-the-fullest baseball team that New York couldn't get enough of. Perhaps that's one of the reasons *Mets Extra* was such a hit; when you are covering the likes of Dwight Gooden, Keith Hernandez, Gary Carter, Mookie Wilson, Lenny Dykstra, Ron Darling, and Darryl Strawberry, well, you're off and running.

Like so many other decisions at WFAN—and in this case WHN, the station that became WFAN—every new program created a forum for talent to develop itself. With *Mets Extra*, that forum was utilized by Rose, and through a trickle-down effect, it also inspired a college kid who came from the first family of sports broadcasting.

"I remember getting a phone call from Howie Rose. I knew Howie from my father and from being around Madison Square Garden at different sporting events. I was a freshman at NYU, and it must have been toward the end of my freshman year," said Kenny Albert, the son of famous New York sportscaster Marv Albert, as well as the nephew of Al Albert and Steve Albert, who also called games on television.

Kenny may have been young, but one thing he did know after growing up with a radio always within earshot—in his neck of Long Island, cable television wasn't available back then—was that he loved radio. He loved the concept of sports on the radio. And even at 18, he was ready to go.

"Howie gave me a call at school and told me he was going to be hosting a show called *Mets Extra*, and asked if I would be interested in being the associate producer for the home games," Albert said. "I obviously jumped at the opportunity. So starting in April '87, I was with Howie at all the Mets home games for the most part.

"Back then, he would stay on until midnight. Many nights, the games would end at 10:00, and one of my duties was to grab whoever the Mets' 'Player of the Game' was, right inside the clubhouse. You'd go in the door, turn right, and there was this equipment mounted on the wall with the headset. I would literally just stand there and wait for the PR people to bring over the star of the game, whether it was Strawberry or Gooden or whomever. We'd do that, then I'd go back to the booth and sit there with Howie for the next two hours. I did that pretty much for the '87, '88, and '89 seasons. Unbelievable learning experience.

"To be there, to be involved with the Mets at the time—just a huge, huge deal. They were a staple. Having Imus, obviously, gave The Fan credibility, and his listeners carried over from the other stations he had been on. But having a very good Mets team—a team that had won the year before in '86 and would go to the playoffs again in '88—having them for 162 games was a big, big deal."

You couldn't go very far in New York in those days without seeing a Mets jersey or hat or jacket. In a town that loves the game of baseball, a city that has witnessed so many magical moments, the Mets were the "it" team in the mid-1980s.

That may be hard to believe for the younger New York sports fans, those baseball upstarts raised on All-Stars Derek Jeter, Mariano Rivera, and five Yankees World Series titles from 1996 to 2009, but it's true. The Mets were the marquee attraction back then. They had style and swagger, long before most athletes even knew what that latter term was.

Which was good for WFAN. The Mets' mojo made for more listeners, more advertising dollars, and better ratings. They were the perfect team for The Fan at the perfect time.

"They loved what the media could do for them. They were very aware of everything around them," said Jeff Pearlman, a former writer at *Sports Illustrated* and author of *The Bad Guys Won*, an unprecedented look at the 1986 Mets. "Hernandez was very in tune to what the media was saying. And Carter? Forget about it. They called him 'Camera Carter.'

"It really was a different era back then. It wasn't like you would go home after games, scan the Internet, and Google yourself to see what people were saying about you. You kind of had to find it a little bit. But [Mets vice president of media relations] Jay Horwitz would cut out their clippings and have them for [the players] every day. So they knew everything that was written and said about them, and they would respond to it.

"One thing that I think is true in relation to radio and the Mets is that radio was kind of a gritty medium back then. Talk radio was like a bunch of Joes—still is in a way. Guys get on there and say 'Such and such sucks,' and 'What the hell is Davey doing?' But that's what the Mets were and kind of still are. The Mets are always gritty and schlubby, even when they were good. You had Hernandez smoking a cigarette in the dugout, and [Wally] Backman and Dykstra being these dirtbags. Radio fit in with that. It allowed Joey from Queens to get on there and say, 'Oh, the fucking Mets this,' or 'The fucking Yankees that.'

"I really feel that FAN came along with the Mets in the '80s and sort of mirrored who they were."

One of the hard-to-quantify effects of WFAN is its impact on the actual teams themselves and the decisions they make. The fans listen, we all know that. The competition checks in as well. But team executives also listen, especially to the marquee shows. Maybe not all of the time, and maybe they take what they hear with a grain of salt. But to think that general managers and front-office bigwigs don't listen to what's being said about their teams on WFAN is a tad naïve.

When talking about the Mets, look no further than the acquisition of All-Star catcher Mike Piazza.

"A lot of people have talked about this, and there's something to it, that [Mike Francesa and Chris Russo] may have been indirectly responsible for Mike Piazza being here," said Rich Ackerman, a long-time update man on WFAN. "That was on all week leading up to the trade. That definitely swayed things."

Piazza was a glamorous, powerful, All-Star catcher with the Dodgers who was traded to the Florida Marlins on May 14, 1998, along with Todd Zeile, for Gary Sheffield, Charles Johnson, Bobby Bonilla, Manuel Barrios, and Jim Eisenreich. But the Marlins weren't intent on keeping Piazza around long term. They wanted to cut salary and start over. So, they almost immediately started taking calls from other teams about Piazza. Whether the Mets were one of those first teams in line, we'll never know. What we do know is they eventually got their man.

"I definitely think that the calls to The Fan, and Mike and Chris talking about Piazza to the Mets, really was a part of it," Ackerman said. "Whether or not the Mets listened to that, I don't know. But I don't think you can deny the fact that people in the Mets front office—at the least—were aware of that. That's just my feeling, but I definitely think that was a big part of it. People called in all week long saying, 'If this guy is available, you have to go get him. Have to!'"

Well, they did. Piazza played in just five games for Florida. And on May 22, he was traded to the Mets for Preston Wilson, Ed Yarnall, and Geoff Goetz. The rest was history. Piazza played for the Mets until 2005, and became the face of the franchise along the way. He hit .296 with 220 home runs and 655 RBIs in his eight years with New York. He played in 972 games and led the Mets to the playoffs in 1999 and 2000, the latter culminating in a trip to the World Series.

Did WFAN play a large role in the Mets' acquisition of Piazza? To be fair, Piazza was a superstar who was making big money and was in line to make even more. In sports, especially in baseball, those types of players often end up in New York anyway. And the Mets were smart enough to clearly identify a player who could help them at the gate, on the field, and in the media. But it is interesting to consider that caller after caller continued to push Piazza to Francesa and Russo, even though he had just been dealt to Florida.

The love affair between the station and the franchise has worked both ways, and as the players were becoming stars in the city, so too, were some of the hosts. At times, the hosts found new fans in unlikely places.

Francesa—back in 1988, even before his days on *Mike and the Mad Dog*—was a perfect example. Some of the Mets were drawn to his style and even his knowledge of, ahem, the point spreads.

Remember, this Mets bunch was a group that liked to push the envelope, and Francesa, who cut his teeth in the business at CBS reporting and producing college sports, was an expert who attracted their attention.

"I had a member of the '88 Mets come over to me on the field during [batting practice] once," Rose said. "He said 'Hey, Howie, this Francesa guy. I've been following his college football picks and have been doing really well. Do you think he'd mind if I called him and picked his brain?'"

The timing of this batting practice conversation on the grass of Shea Stadium deserves a mention. The Mets were about to square off with the Los Angeles Dodgers in a National League Championship Series game in October of 1988. But, hey, that's college football season, too. Far be it for a national event like the NLCS to interfere with a player's gaming hobby, right?

"I said, 'You're playing a fucking game in the league championship series! Do you really need to be thinking about this now?'" Rose said. "But I told Mike, and he said 'Oh, yeah, sure, have him call me.' I'll never forget that one."

There's a comfort level that good beat journalists reach with the players they cover. Rose certainly reached it with the Mets, and so has Ed Coleman, an original at WFAN who has been the station's beat reporter for the Mets through many tough seasons.

"It's a little bit of a juggling act," Coleman said, when asked about the process of compiling information, conversing with superstars in good times and bad, and deciding what he should and shouldn't report to The Fan's audience. "I tell all the players, 'Hey, I'm going to be here every day. I'm here.' Some I don't have to tell that to. Some guys get it right away. There are guys like David Wright and [John] Franco and [Al] Leiter who get it.

"But there are others who are skeptical or wary about the press. But if you're there every day, they obviously become more comfortable with you. And again, if they're a little hesitant, you bring up that point again: 'I'll be here every day. If you have a shitty game, I'm going to say you had a shitty game. That's it. It's not personal. But if something I say bothers you or is not right, just come to me because I'll be here every day.'

"There are talk show hosts who will sit back there in an ivory tower and shoot arrows and never come to the ballpark and never come to the locker room. I think that's why a lot of athletes in general resent talk radio. When you're in the trenches with the guys, if you're straight with them, they'll be okay with you. There are going to be times where, hey, you have to criticize people, and you have to criticize teams and organizations. It's just the way it is. Like I said, I always make it pretty clear to them that I'm here, and that they can come to me. I'm not hiding."

Sweeny Murti feels the same way. A former intern and producer at WFAN who worked his way through the ranks and is now the station's beat reporter for the Yankees, Murti runs through the same paces as Coleman but talks to different faces. "I always think of my job as criticizing the performance, if needed, and not the player," he said. "You have to talk to the Yankees in those terms, guys like Derek Jeter, because they are very aware when the light is on."

The Coleman-Murti duo is a terrific luxury for a radio station to have—two dedicated journalists in a baseball-mad town—and it's helped to keep The Fan ahead of everyone else.

Murti, who picked up the Yankees beat in 2001, has witnessed and reported on memorable games, colorful characters, unforgettable stories, and even a World Series title in 2009. Let's face it, the Yankees are the Yankees. But at The Fan, it's still a Mets world.

"We've been known as the Mets' station for such a long time," Murti said. "That's what people know. Every night, unless there is something *really* happening with the Yankees, I think there are more Mets fans that call than Yankees fans. There are a lot of Mets fans out there, more than the team gets credit for, and this is where they go, this is where they call.

"I mean, look at our station logo. Our logo is orange and blue, and we've patterned ourselves around our affiliation with the Mets. And that has withstood the test of time."

There are also a large number of Mets fans working at the station. Among The Fan's current daily lineup, Boomer Esiason, Craig Carton, Evan Roberts, Joe Benigno, and Steve Somers all support the team from Queens.

In the end, the talent at The Fan shares an obvious love for New York sports, so you can't blame them for showing their true colors. It's why they battled to break through in this business. And it's why they battle through those tough times to continue living the dream.

Every so often, they are rewarded with the privilege of witnessing true gems—special moments from special players that will live forever. Many such events have been broadcast on WFAN over the past 26 years, and fortunately for Rose, he's been at the forefront of quite a few.

Remember, Rose was one of those young, die-hard Mets fans sitting in the upper deck at Shea Stadium decades ago. A dreamer longing for a way to get closer to the action. Well, he succeeded... and then some. And on June 1, 2012, against the backdrop of 27,609 screaming fans at Citi Field, the Mets' new home, he was rewarded with making a momentous call in one of the proudest moments in franchise history.

And now Santana, perhaps a strike away. Johan sweeps a little dirt away from the left of the pitching rubber. Steps behind the rubber, tugs once at the bill of his cap, takes a deep breath, and steps to the third base side of the rubber.

Santana into the windup, the payoff pitch on the way...swung and missed! Strike three! He's done it! Johan Santana has pitched a no-hitter, in the 8,020[th] game in the history of the New York Mets! They finally have a no-hitter! And who better to do it than Johan Santana, and what a remarkable story!

His teammates are mobbing him at the mound! The players in the bullpen are trotting in! It is a surreal feeling here at Citi Field! The first no-hitter in the history of the New York Mets has been pitched by as worthy a candidate as anyone! Johan Santana, put it in the books! The history books! One of the seminal moments in the history of this franchise!

The call was perfect in so many ways. It captured both the moment and the Mets' decades-long quest for a baseball achievement that so many other franchises experience quite often. In 50 years of baseball in Queens, the Mets came close a few times, but never had a no-hitter.

So, for Rose, it was a surreal feeling to watch Santana's 3-2 changeup draw a swing and a miss from St. Louis third baseman David Freese, finishing off an 8–0 Mets victory.

"First of all, I remember saying on the air that night that it was *not* going to be the night, because he had walked five, I think, in total," Rose said. "I said, 'Well, if you're thinking tonight's going to be the night, forget it.' [Mets manager Terry Collins] had made such a fuss about the pitch count and not getting [Santana] past 110, and because he was going to sail past that, I didn't think there was any way in the world he'd be allowed to make a bid for a no-hitter. I kept on thinking, *It's never going to happen.* And it happened. When he struck Freese out, I was in shock. I was in absolute utter disbelief that it had actually happened.

"The thing that I'm proudest about of the call is that I didn't say 'Put it in the books' [Rose's famous catchphrase] for about 60 seconds.

It didn't even dawn on me because the enormity of the moment is such that you just report, report, report. What do you see? What are the players doing? Where are they coming from? Players coming out of the bullpen. Players coming out of the dugout. And then it just dawned on me: Oh, yeah, 'Put it in the books! The history books!' And I'm actually quite proud of that because I think age, maturity, and experience tell you in moments like that to not start screaming incoherently at strike three. You have to describe the scene."

Rose has gotten used to this big-time, big-event frame of mind for WFAN. After all, in 1994, while the play-by-play man for the New York Rangers, he authored one of the greatest sports radio calls in history.

> Fetisov, for the Devils, plays it cross-ice, into the far corner. Matteau swoops in to intercept. Matteau behind the net, swings it in front. He scores! *Matteau! Matteau! Matteau*! Stephane Matteau! And the Rangers have one more hill to climb, baby! But it's Mount Vancouver! The Rangers are headed to the Finals!

Rose's enthusiastic, efficient, effervescent call of Stephane Matteau's game-winning goal in Game 7 of the NHL Eastern Conference Finals against the New Jersey Devils set the stage for the Rangers' Stanley Cup championship—one that was 54 years in the making—and was the apex of a rewarding time at WFAN. The station, at the time, owned the broadcasting rights to the Rangers and the New York Knicks, who made a run to the NBA Finals that same spring.

"You're talking about the heyday of the station. Spring of 1994, Knicks and Rangers playing big games, and the Yankees were on the cusp of winning in 1996. Everyone turned to The Fan, and we were everywhere," Murti said. "Pregames, postgames, remotes—we wrapped ourselves around those runs and took the city for a ride. Everyone got caught up in it."

Rose certainly did.

"I've got to be honest with you, it might be the greatest call I've ever heard in sports," ESPN New York's Don La Greca, now a broadcaster for the Rangers, said of Rose's call. "Because as an aspiring play-by-play guy, it had all of the elements. Nobody was more on top of it than Howie."

Everyone in New York remembers that call, not just hockey fans. It proves how important professional teams can be for a radio station, and Rose, who is now the television voice of the rival New York Islanders, will always cherish that.

"As I left the building, as happy as I was that they had won, I was a little nervous as to how the call was going to be accepted," Rose said. "So, I leave the Garden and there's a guy in his car, sitting on 33rd Street, and he yells out, 'Howie, great call. Great call.' And I just think he's being nice because he saw me and he's glad they won. But then I get into my car and I'm listening to The Fan on the way home, and they're replaying the call every five minutes. Every five minutes! And people were talking about the call as much as they were the game and the series! It was Steve Somers, and I will never forget it.

"The next day, it was Russ Salzberg on The Fan, and he's taking calls, and that's all that everyone was talking about. As I was driving to Shea the next morning I was listening to the callers, and I finally thought to myself, *Maybe that call wasn't so bad after all.* It's just incredible to me how it has endured for so many years. It's just very, very flattering."

Perhaps that's the power of The Fan, too. People listen to important calls. People remember important calls. And there's been plenty on this proud station. Take the NFL's Giants, for example. Lost in all of the Rangers and Mets drama, it's easy to forget that Big Blue eventually hooked up with The Fan and won two Super Bowls (2008 and 2012) on Sports Radio 66's air.

But at the end of the day, the Mets have cast the largest shadow in WFAN history. As Rose recalled all those wonderful memories, he kept returning to Santana's special night in Queens.

After Rose concluded his on-air duties that evening, there was still time to savor the moment. The man who once walked down the steps of Shea Stadium's upper deck in the 1960s as a kid now made his way down to the clubhouse of Citi Field. It had been a long journey for the broadcaster, the pitcher, and the team. And it made for a superb ending to a special night.

"I went into the clubhouse—this is about 90 minutes after the final out—and I was hoping Johan would still be there. And he was, because they had him signing every artifact possible, for obvious reasons. But it was great. I walked into the clubhouse and nobody was there except Johan and a couple of the clubhouse kids," Rose recalled.

"And I went over to him and gave him a big hug, and I said, 'You know, I've never actually cried on the air. But, man, I've got to tell you, I almost broke up there in the ninth inning a little bit.' And he got a little excited about it. He said 'Did you cry?' I said 'No,'" and he was a little disappointed.

"But, yeah, the little kid in me was back. The kid in the upper deck. I asked him to sign the scorecard. I have a book that I keep, night in and night out, as opposed to separate score sheets or score-cards. It's all in a book. So I asked him to sign the scorebook.

"And really, that's as good as it gets for me."

For millions of Mets fans nationwide—a proud, passionate group that is underrated in not only its volume but its loyalty—the feeling was mutual, Howie.

And it was all captured on WFAN.

9

The Most Interesting Man in the World

Ian Eagle was Mike Francesa and Chris Russo's producer early on. When [former WFAN program director] Eric Spitz got married, I was in Portland, Maine, for a hockey game, and I left the game early and flew in for the wedding. Eric said, 'I'll have one of the other guys from the station, a young guy, a great guy, pick you up at the airport.' It was Ian Eagle. I think it was the first time that we had met. He picked me up at LaGuardia and we drove out to Long Island, so it was probably 45 minutes. I wish I could tell you what we talked about. One thing I do know, it was definitely about sports. And with Ian, it was definitely entertaining. —KENNY ALBERT

IN A BUSINESS LOADED WITH EGOS, with broadcasters ready, willing, and able to step on another broadcaster on their way to the top, it's rare that you find someone who *everybody* likes.

There are passionate, professional personalities all over the industry—especially at WFAN—who have many more friends than enemies. But keep in mind, this is a dog-eat-dog business. At some point along the line, most of these talents have run into someone who they just didn't connect with, someone who they just didn't get along with.

When it comes to the case Ian Eagle, good luck finding *that* someone.

"Ian Eagle? Wonderful. Just a wonderful professional, and of course, extremely talented. Of all the guys at The Fan, I'll tell you this: when I go through my off-the-field stuff, the guy that I speak to most and the guy that's quick to text or call is Ian. I don't think anybody knows that. Just a genuine human being who cares about everyone."

Those were the words of Sid Rosenberg, a WFAN alum who has run into his share of issues. He has sometimes said the wrong things. Other times, he's *done* the wrong things. Clearly, he is one such talent who has an enemy or two. But through it all—the chemical addiction, the arrest for DUI, the gaffes on air—Rosenberg can always count on Eagle.

So, of course, like seemingly everyone else in the business, Rosenberg can share a story or two about Eagle, a former WFAN Mr. Do It All, who has since developed into one of the nation's premier television and radio play-by-play broadcasters. But it goes well beyond the moral support factor and the "Here For You When You Need It" mentality that helps to define Eagle's personality. In fact, that is just one of several layers to Eagle.

Indeed, Ian—pronounced "Eye-an" and not the standard "Eee-an"—has made connections in every pocket of the business... and kept all of them. He's the kid in school who walks down the hall and gets stopped by everyone—students, teachers, janitors, you name it. He is the quarterback, the prom king, and the valedictorian, all in one. If there was a race for class president at Sports Broadcasting High, he'd win it going away. In short—and that's no knock on him, because he *is* short—he could possibly challenge the Dos Equis Man for the title of "The Most Interesting Man in the World."

Never afraid to poke fun at himself of course—stick around him long enough, and you'll hear the story of how people always ask him, "Is that your real name? Is it Iron Eagle, like the movie?"—he always sports a smile. It's usually preceded by a joke or two. And through it all—on air and off—he always says and does the right things.

Forget Dos Equis. Shoot, the personality known around the business as "The Birdman" may actually be Tim Tebow deep down inside.

"Ian Eagle always gave me advice, he was always one of the guys I could rely on," said Marc Malusis, an overnight host on WFAN. "Ian always said to me, 'As long as you're on the air, you're good. Continue to work at your craft and your art form.' He's right about that. You want to consistently get better at what you do, you don't want to get stagnant. I think I've improved year in and year out because of insight like that.

"And that's just Ian for you. That's who he is. He's a mentor, and everything he does—and everything he preaches—is for greater cause of being successful."

Eagle knows a little about success. He was destined for it as a teenager, even before he enrolled at Syracuse University. He knew, long before arriving on campus, what he wanted. He knew how to get it. And he knew that no one was going to stop him from getting it.

"I had a clear idea of what I wanted to do at an early age. Probably by eight or nine, I knew I wanted to be a sports broadcaster and I was fortunate when I told my father, and he said 'Well, that's what you'll do.' No second guessing, no questioning of 'Why wouldn't you go into a more stable career?' My dad was an entertainer, a stand-up comedian, an actor, a musician. And my mom was an entertainer, as well. So clearly they didn't look at normal 9-to-5 jobs as the way their son had to go," Eagle recalled. "So with that in mind, I went to Syracuse with the clear objective to be in *this* business. And WFAN started just before my sophomore year. The timing could not be any better. I clearly remember listening to the station and being in awe that this was something that you could do! My level of expectations prior to that was you're either a sports anchor or a play-by-play man. The idea of doing full-time sports talk was not even on the radar.

"So, that really changed things for me and it gave me something to shoot for. It was no longer a theory. It was real. It was tangible. When I came home during vacations, I could listen to *all-sports radio*. So, being a student of not only broadcasting but a student of the industry, I was trying to soak up as much as I possibly could during that time. I was fortunate to get an internship between my junior and senior year at WFAN, and that was life-changing. It was really my first real exposure to a professional environment and it was just when the station started to come into its own."

So, with his eyes wide open, Eagle set forth on his WFAN journey in the summer of 1989. He would never be the same.

"The goal with any internship is to observe, to come away from the experience feeling as if you've learned something and I certainly did. That was really important in my development. It gave me a baseline to work off of. I remember vividly going back my senior year really confident I had knowledge that others *didn't* have, and my senior year at Syracuse went very well. I was doing a lot of games, doing a lot of different broadcasts, and felt as if I had an upper hand based on WFAN," Eagle said. "I get a call in February of my senior year from The Fan. It was fairly early for college students. It was nine in the morning. I was still sleeping. The phone woke me up and Barry Loberfeld, who was [WFAN program director] Mark Mason's assistant, said 'Hey, Ian, we have a job opening for a producer's slot. Would you like to interview for it?'

"So over spring break, I went to interview. I called Eric Spitz, who was a producer, and asked him, 'Hey, what's the story?' He said, 'Well, look you're probably not going to get this job, but it's really important to go through the process and at the very least, you'll have gotten some experience.'

"Now, I'm not even sure I *want* the job. I had an opportunity to go to Buffalo and be on the air, and West Virginia. But I go for the interview. I meet with Mark Mason and we hit it off. He asked me when I could start and I say I graduate May 10. I said I could start... May 13? He said, 'Well, great,' and that's how we left it. I walked out of the interview. I spoke with Eric for a minute, who was working that day. He said 'How'd it go?' I said I think it went really well, and he chuckled and said 'Okay, I'll talk to you in a couple weeks once this process settles down.' I went back to my father's house in Forest Hills. I'm getting ready to pack my car and head back to Syracuse and the phone rings.

"My father picks it up, tells me Eric Spitz is on the phone, and he says '*WHAT THE HELL DID YOU SAY TO MARK?*' I said, 'Did I offend him? What are you talking about?' He goes 'No, he wants to offer you the job. He wants to hire you.' I said 'I *told* you it went very well,' and he said, 'What are you going to do? Do you want this job?' At that point, I guess it hit me the idea of working at WFAN was more important than being on the air somewhere else, and I said to him 'Yeah, I want the job.'

"So, I get there and I was the producer for seven-to-midnight which included *Mets Extra*, [WFAN primetime host] Howie Rose's show, Knicks and Rangers' broadcasts, and I worked out of the studio. I was told in no uncertain terms that if I had aspirations to be on the air, I should put those to the side because it's *not* going to happen. I accepted those terms and thought in the back of my mind *Let me get into the day-to-day flow of the station and we'll see what happens down the road.*

"That was that. No post-graduation stuff here. No backpacking through Europe. Nothing. I literally graduated on a Friday and started work on a Monday. I was thrilled. But in the back of my mind, I felt I needed to get an opportunity to be on the air."

He was right. And it shouldn't come as any surprise. Anyone who has that vivid a memory, and that passionate a determination, was bound to reach a WFAN microphone. He is, after all, a story-teller—did you figure that out yet?—and those types usually end up on the air.

"September of 1991, things changed. Stan Martin, sports director at the time, who made the schedule, set the stage. It was a Friday, I was in my cubicle in the newsroom preparing for *Mets Extra* and Stan is on the telephone. Stan came from a dramatic background. He was an actor, and often would treat the newsroom like it was a theatre. So all you would hear is one side of the phone conversations. Loudly. The phone rings, he picks it up and all you hear is '*WHAT? NO! REALLY? NO! YOU'VE GOT TO BE KIDDING ME! NO! OK!*' And he hangs up.

"He turns to me and—he didn't even call me by my name—he just said '*YOU! YOU WANT TO BE ON THE AIR, DON'T CHA?*' I turned to him, nodded my head and said 'Yes.' He said 'Go write a sportscast and make a tape, and bring me the tape.' I said why, and he said '*JUST DO IT, MAN!*' I have no idea why he's yelling at me! But I run and write a sportscast. I grabbed some sound from the rack. He said '*ONE TAKE! NOT TWO TAKES! ONE TAKE. AND HAND ME THE TAPE!*'

"I did the sportscast, handed him the tape. And I'm just sitting in the newsroom. I have no idea what's going on. He comes back and he says '*YOU'RE ON THE SCHEDULE SUNDAY! MY UPDATE GUY HAS PNEUMONIA!*' And that was it. I did a Sunday update shift during the NFL and then I was on the schedule the next week. I was given an overnight shift here and there, and [former WFAN reporter and now ESPN anchor] Steve Levy and I hosted a five-hour Super Bowl pregame show before Buffalo and Washington [in 1992]. Before I knew it, I was put on the *Mike and the Mad Dog* shift.

"But I also was given the duties of overnight host from midnight to 6:00 AM Friday and midnight to 6:00 AM Saturday into Sunday. And that's really where I was given an opportunity to make the most of my time. I was never told 'You're inexperienced. You don't have enough reps.' They just gave me a shot."

And he aced it. As a New Yorker, he could feel the pain and the joy of callers. He knew their feelings, related well to them, and responded in kind. And as a developing professional, obviously, he was also hitting it off at the station.

"First of all, he brought bagels to work. That's always going to go over well in radio: free food," said Spitz, who recalled some early Mets pregame shows, where Eagle would arrive with breakfast. "On those days, we called it *Mets Eggstra*. But Ian was there with bagels, a nice touch."

Eagle soon developed a strong bond with Chris Russo, as well, one half of the *Mike and the Mad Dog* burgeoning empire that was quickly taking over sports radio.

"Mike and Chris really liked Ian, they saw a lot of potential in him," said Sweeny Murti, WFAN's Yankees beat reporter. "Mike and Chris didn't like everyone, we all know that. They picked their spots here and there. But they both liked Ian a lot."

Russo sides with people he truly likes deep down inside, those with talent and upside, and those who just have *it*, whatever *it* is. Eagle was one of those.

"I'm happy to hear that," Russo said when learning of the influence he had on Eagle. "Ian was a kid. Bright. Eager. And I related to him. I enjoyed being around him. I lived in the city. Ian lived in the city, so he drove me home every night."

Eagle indeed became a chauffeur, and learned even more while toting Russo around the Big Apple.

"I would say looking back on that time, Chris and I grew very close on a personal level. The driving was key," Eagle said. "It actually worked to my advantage. I enjoyed his company but it also got me out of work a half hour earlier! So I did have some personal gain in driving him home. He went to the boss and said 'Hey, I really need Ian to leave when I leave, when the show ends.' I was supposed to stay on for another half hour. So much for that!

"But we definitely connected. I was recently engaged. I had a lot of things happening in my life, and Chris was trying to deal with the fame and everything that comes along with being a successful media star. And he knew that our conversations would stay between us. What I relayed to him—of course, later on—was that our conversations didn't necessarily stay in his head. Despite what we said beforehand—what is said in the car stays in the car—my stories would make their way on air! He couldn't help himself. He had no filter."

That's Russo for you. Longtime update man Rich Ackerman, in fact, lived by the credo "Don't tell Chris anything you don't want on the air. He'll blurt it right out."

But what happened to Ian—as Mad Dog delivered some of his stories—was that the Eagle brand was being pushed to the masses. Russo, indirectly, was promoting Eagle and telling all of New York more about him. Whether it seemed right or not, it helped the profile.

"Looking back on that time, I really was the first true product of the radio station. I had no other professional experience. The only world of broadcasting I knew was based on WFAN. So all of my training, all of my insight, came from being around that station," Eagle said. "So to say I was a product of sports radio would be too general. I was absolutely a direct product of WFAN radio. What that meant, really, in those days was having an opinion and speaking with conviction and being able to get on the air and make a show move along. Even at a young age—I graduated college at 21; I had skipped a grade as a kid so I was always a year younger—I got to WFAN and it might have been blind confidence more than anything else that I believed I could do it."

Again, he wasn't alone. People—in and out of the station— noticed. Before too long, WFAN couldn't even hold down The Birdman much longer. Clearly, there were other mediums to soar to.

"I was sitting at my desk at Channel 9 and I get a call from Ian Eagle. The radio job opened up with the [New Jersey] Nets and I was connected with the Nets. I knew the management. I knew the brass. At that time, the president was Jon Spoelstra," said Russ Salzberg, a sports anchor at WWOR Channel 9 and a former midday host at WFAN. "Anyway, I get a call from Ian...'Russ, I got to get this job.' I said, 'Okay, what's up?' He said, 'I know it's available.' I hung the phone up with him and called Jon Spoelstra...and they were ready to make a move. They even had a guy from the [Continental Basketball Association] at the time—and I said, 'Look, Ian's really good. You know who he is. Just hear his tape.' I call Ian right back [and say] 'You need to get the tape over there right now. I mean *right now*.'"

The "right now" part was never a problem for Eagle. He didn't get to the premier sports radio station at such an early age without having a sense of urgency. If he had to deliver something to someone in the hope of landing an NBA radio play-by-play gig—a plateau only a handful of broadcasters in this country will ever experience—he was going to get it there faster than FedEx. The interesting angle in this instance, however, was the actual material to deliver. He had a tape, sure. But he needed more.

"So I call the Nets director of broadcasting, Amy Scheer," Eagle said. "I cold-call her and explained I'm Ian Eagle from WFAN radio, saw there's an opening and would be very interested. She told me 'Look, we're very late in the process. You're getting in here late. But if you want to drop something off here at the offices, I'll take a listen.'

"Well, that was 1994. I had not done play-by-play since my senior year of college which was 1990, but I had a tape of Syracuse–Seton Hall played at the Meadowlands. I thought maybe that was good karma [because the Nets, at the time, played in the Meadowlands, as well]. So, I grabbed the tape, drove it over. Amy met me down in the lobby in East Rutherford, New Jersey, and took the tape. She said 'Look I'll give you a call, let you know.' Two days later, she called me. She said 'I played it for my boss, [executive vice president] Jim Lampariello. He liked it but he'd like to hear something more recent.'

"And I'm thinking to myself *More recent?* I don't have anything *more recent!* That's all I got. She said 'Can you bring me something *more recent?*' So, knowing I had absolutely nothing *more recent*, of course I said...ABSOLUTELY! So I went to NBA Entertainment. A guy by the name of Rich Kopilnick had reached out to me a couple years earlier to see if I could do a voiceover for the NBA. He was a contact. So, long story short, I called him and I said 'Look, is there any way to put me in a room and just record me doing a Nets game off television and mix in crowd noise?' He said...'Uh, yeah, we can probably figure that out. Just come over.'

"So I went in. I called a Knicks-Nets playoff game from that year off a monitor. They mixed in crowd noise. I went over to Scheer's, dropped the tape off, and she called me back the following week and said 'Our team president wants to meet you.' That's Jon Spoelstra, whose son eventually became the coach of the Miami Heat, Erik.

"So, that's great, but Amy tells me 'We have one other person and basically it's going to be his job unless something changes drastically in the interview process.' I said 'Can I ask you who it is out of curiosity?' And she told me it was a guy by the name of Bill Roberts. She said 'You wouldn't know him, he does play-by-play in Yakima [Washington] for the CBA.' And I didn't say it to her, but I *knew* him. He did one year of graduate work in Syracuse. And I thought to myself, *Okay, if it is down to me and Bill Roberts, I've got a 50-50 shot.* So I go in for the interview, meet with Jon. Very nice guy."

And it's at this point where you see the true essence of Eagle rising to the surface. Here was a young broadcaster who had already proven, in this job search alone, that he was willing to do anything. So, he put all his chips on the table.

"Rolled the dice. I said to Jon, 'Look, I plan on doing a lot of different things in this business and I think I'm going to be able to achieve some great things down the line. If I get this job, for the rest of my life, they will mention *Nets play-by-play man* and you'll be the reason why.'"

The bold Birdman.

"That can go one of two ways. Either the interviewer can think that you're pompous and kick you out of the office, or it could pique their interest, which in his case I think it did. I left the office. I actually went on vacation for my one-year anniversary with my wife to San Francisco and I got a call on my answering machine at home—this is pre–cell phone days—and it was Amy from the Nets. 'Please give me a call.'

"And so I called from San Francisco and she told me I had gotten the job. It was about a three-week process that obviously changed my life, changed my career. It was really one of the biggest breaks that I could have asked for. But they told me I would have to leave WFAN to do the job, which I said, 'I understand.'"

But the karma behind this whole transaction was too perfect for it to end like that. Surely, there was a way to get the best of both worlds, right?

"I went to Joel Hollander, the general manager of the station. 'Look, I've got this opportunity.' He said 'Ah, that's a great move!' I said 'Part of the issue was Mr. Spoelstra told me I would have to leave WFAN to do this job.' He said, 'Well, that's silly.'"

Turns out, Hollander contacted the Nets to undo this "silly" little rule.

"He picks up the phone, calls the Nets, and says 'Jon Spoelstra, please.' And within 15 seconds, he says 'Joel Hollander, FAN. Jon, how ya doing? Look, I heard you hired Ian Eagle, one of our guys. Congratulations. He's a great kid.' He said 'Let me ask you something, though. Why wouldn't you also want him to be on WFAN while doing your games? That's only going to be more publicity for you. He's going to go on the air, I'm sure he's going to take Nets calls. Nets fans are going to call in. What do you think?'

"Of course, that's Hollander I'm hearing, nothing else. He says... 'Uh huh. Okay. Great. We'll see ya.' He hangs up the phone and says 'Nope, you're fine! That's it. You can stay.' And that was it. I was able to do both. If the original plan was in place, I would have left WFAN entirely in 1994."

And so began a career in multitasking that continues to this day. Eagle has truly become of the great jugglers of this industry where you can literally see or hear him doing one sport in one city on one night, and see or hear him in a totally different city, doing a different sport, on the next.

"I couldn't have been happier for him," Salzberg said. "First off, I think he's absolutely terrific at what he does. It's not because I have an affection for the guy, I think he's *really, really* good. There's a bunch of stories like that in the Naked City; how people get started and what not. Ian's done very well for himself. He's busted his ass and everything he has, he deserves."

But Eagle was not fit to stop at NBA radio play-by-play. Tremendous experience notwithstanding, there were other sports, other mediums to tackle. And of course, along the way, there were more Eagle stories.

"I am amazed at what he can do, how he fits it all in," said Evan Roberts, The Fan's resident Nets die-hard. "When I think of Ian, I think of the Nets, he is the voice of the Nets. Period. But he does so much more, and gets to so many places. I really don't know how he does it."

Three years after landing the Nets position, he graduated to the NFL. He didn't need to run to another office to make a tape this time. His body of work had blossomed to where it was just a matter of time before another job surfaced. And it did. And then *another one* did.

"And it didn't take long for Ian Eagle to make those amazing leaps," WFAN operations manager Mark Chernoff said. "From an intern to a board operator to hosting shows to doing pro games. Just a great talent."

The New York Jets were still on WFAN, and after four years of doing pre- and postgame shows, the club thought it was time to move Eagle up the broadcasting ladder again. In 1997, he became Gang Green's radio play-by-play man.

"It was [former Jets coach] Bill Parcells' first year. They were coming off of a 1–15 season," Eagle said. "I was going to grow with the team. It was perfect timing."

And isn't that just the story of his broadcasting life? Right place, right time. Before too long, Eagle, an underrated fashionista, acquired a famous CBS blazer—"Ahh yes, I love that jacket."—and worked the NCAA tournament. That led to NFL play-by-play on that national network.

There are so many skills CBS fell in love with, and they're the same that WFAN, the Nets, and the Jets saw way back when: An incredible handle on every game; coasting through the ebbs and flows; a second-to-none chemistry with his partners, no matter how much or little they work together; and just the right emphasis and tone to any style of play. Also, there's the Eagle staple—just the right touch of pop culture, humor, and a sense of real life.

That carries away from CBS, as well, and onto the YES Network, the television home of the Nets where Eagle now calls NBA games. Consider a ho-hum game against Detroit last season. The struggling Pistons shouldn't have challenged these talented Nets on this night. But they did, taking the home team down to the wire on December 14, 2012. But eventually, Joe Johnson nailed a jumper as time expired in a second overtime session, ending a dramatic 107–105 win that Eagle captured as only he can.

In that first NBA season in Brooklyn, there were plenty of star appearances in the stands. On this night, comedian Jerry Seinfeld was front and center, and the YES cameras showcased him several times. One such time, was right after Johnson's winner. Seinfeld, like most everyone else in Barclays Center, was ecstatic over the result.

So Eagle tipped his cap to *Seinfeld*, one of America's great television sitcoms, and quoted a line from a 1993 episode to describe the winner. The line was from "The Implant" in which guest star Teri Hatcher's breasts were a theme. She closes a scene by walking out of Seinfeld's apartment, and in referring to her breasts, she says, "And by the way. They're real…and they're spectacular."

Cue Ian.

"Four seconds left, double overtime, Nets looking for the win. Johnson, the step back…he buries it! Joe Johnson! He wins it in double overtime!"

It's at this point, when Seinfeld is shown on YES with a smile from ear to ear.

"That was REAL," Eagle exclaimed, spur of the moment, off the top of his head, unscripted, "and that was...SPECTACULAR!"

Sorta like his career.

10

Mourning and Morning

When Mike [Francesa] and Chris [Russo] broke up, it was
sort of a long illness. When Imus left, it was a short illness.
There was conversation around the newsroom about what
the station was going to do when Imus retired. But there
was never an answer because it was sort of hypothetical.
We never thought it was going to actually happen. It's like
he got hit by a truck and that was it. DOA. It happened so
suddenly, and it was definitely shocking. —ERIC SPITZ

ERIC SPITZ, LIKE SO MANY IN THE RADIO BUSINESS, grew up
on Don Imus. It was a generational thing for several New Yorkers.
Not only do fathers pass teams down to their sons, they also can
bequeath radio personalities to them. And for Spitz, who would go
onto carve a sparkling yet unheralded career as a program director
at WFAN, the father indeed influenced Imus on the son.

"For me, he is *the* reason I got into the business. My dad was a
huge Imus fan—listened to every minute of every broadcast, and was
also a contest winner. My dad would win various contests on what

was then WNBC. Sixty-six McDonald's Egg McMuffins, 66 Arby's specialty sandwiches, you name it. I think my cholesterol is so high because my dad would win those prizes on a regular basis," said Spitz, now the director of programming at the CBS Sports Radio Network.

"So, he developed a relationship with Imus' producer. In one conversation after my father won a contest, he mentioned that he had a son that was a freshman in college that was looking for an internship; that I was working at the college station and had an interest. My dad got some WNBC information, passed it to me, and that was my first internship.

"Without Imus, I don't know if I *ever* get in."

The Spitzes, who used to record Imus' shows on cassettes, are an extreme case, but Don had *that* kind of an effect on New Yorkers. He was mesmerizing, polarizing, and above all others in the morning game, he was addictive. Once he had you, you were hooked.

Which made it so hard to comprehend the end of Imus on WFAN. Retire, leave for another station, try a new medium, you can list options all day, you still weren't going to find many New Yorkers who gave serious thought to the Imus Era ever really ending at The Fan.

Unless, of course, he screwed up. Unless, of course, he went too far. Unless, of course, the unimaginable happened. Well, on April 4, 2007, all of that occurred.

Imus and his crew were talking March Madness on that ill-fated morning, but the men's game wasn't the centerpiece. The women's Final Four was, and sports radio in New York would never be the same. The broadcast was also simulcast on MSNBC. So, when the team began to talk about the Rutgers Scarlet Knights and their appearance in the NCAA tournament title game, a stunned nation listened:

Imus: So, I watched the basketball game last night between—a little bit of Rutgers and Tennessee, the women's final.

[Sports update man] Sid Rosenberg: Yeah, Tennessee won last night—seventh championship for [Tennessee coach] Pat Summitt, I-Man. They beat Rutgers by 13 points.

Imus: That's some rough girls from Rutgers. Man, they got tattoos and—

[Executive producer] Bernard McGuirk: Some hardcore hos.

Imus: That's some nappy-headed hos there. I'm gonna tell you that now, man, that's some—woo. And the girls from Tennessee, they all look cute, you know, so, like—kinda like—I don't know.

McGuirk: A Spike Lee thing.

Imus: Yeah.

McGuirk: The Jigaboos vs. the Wannabes—that movie that he had.

Imus: Yeah, it was a tough—

[News anchor] Charles McCord: *Do the Right Thing.*

McGuirk: Yeah, yeah, yeah.

Imus: I don't know if I'd have wanted to beat Rutgers or not, but they did, right?

Rosenberg: It was a tough watch. The more I look at Rutgers, they look exactly like the Toronto Raptors.

Imus: Well, I guess, yeah.

[Program engineer] Lou Rufino: Only tougher.

McGuirk: The [Memphis] Grizzlies would be more appropriate.

And just like that, *the* line had been crossed. Talking about women in *that* manner, in *that* time and era, was just too much for even the I-Man. Just a patch that lasted a few seconds of radio air ultimately brought the end for Imus at WFAN.

During a weeklong controversy—the New York tabloids ran with the story, Rutgers held a press conference, civil rights leaders did the same, and Imus' face was out there on every platform possible—a move *had* to be made. Imus issued a written apology, of course. He had to. But it didn't put out this fire. It couldn't.

"I want to take a moment to apologize for an insensitive and ill-conceived remark we made the other morning regarding the Rutgers women's basketball team, which lost to Tennessee in the NCAA championship game on Tuesday," Imus wrote. "It was completely inappropriate and we can understand why people were offended. Our characterization was thoughtless and stupid, and we are sorry."

Didn't matter. On April 12, CBS, the parent company of WFAN, let the I-Man go.

"From the outset, I believe all of us have been deeply upset and revulsed by the statements that were made on our air about the young women who represented Rutgers University in the NCAA women's basketball championship with such class, energy, and talent," Leslie Moonves, CBS president and CEO, said at the time.

"Those who have spoken with us the last few days represent people of goodwill from all segments of our society—all races, economic groups, men and women alike. In our meetings with concerned groups, there has been much discussion of the effect language like this has on our young people, particularly young women of color trying to make their way in this society. That consideration has weighed most heavily on our minds as we made our decision, as have the many emails, phone calls, and personal discussions we have had with our colleagues across the CBS Corporation and our many other constituencies."

It was one of very few ugly periods for WFAN. And it gave most everyone affiliated with the station a feeling of uneasiness.

"It was a tough time losing Imus because he and I had been together since 1993," WFAN operations manager Mark Chernoff said. "That's 14 years, and he and I got along great. He was and is such an icon in radio.

"And at the time, we had just signed Imus to a new deal. And Imus had said to me then, 'You know, this might be my last deal.' And

I said, 'Yeah, sure.' But just the fact that he said that to me, it did put it in my head. But I figured I had four or five more years to cross that bridge. So, the incident really sped up the process. It was stunning."

Chris Carlin concurs. An aspiring broadcaster who was working his way up the WFAN food chain, Carlin was working as an update man for Imus, but he was also a play-by-play man for Rutgers. So, in the middle of this treacherous freeway of slipshod strife, Carlin was stuck in traffic.

You see, Carlin had a lot of people in his corner at WFAN, and with reason. He's a jovial, fun-loving guy, who gets along with others. He can also make fun of himself, and that goes over well. So, as he was building his brand at The Fan, Imus—like Mike Francesa and Chris Russo—helped.

"Imus was good to me. He was not an easy guy to work for and it was clearly the most pressure I felt in my life. There was pressure to be funny, pressure to be good. I just think I'm a guy with a decent sense of humor and I just tried to go on his shows, and be prepared to be funny," Carlin said. "Honestly, at times I felt like a square peg in a round hole. I never felt fully comfortable with that show. I think it was just because here's an icon of broadcasting. Here's a bunch of guys who knew what they were doing and I'm just stepping in to do sports. When I really enjoyed doing that show the most was when I could just be myself. When I was trying too hard to prepare something, it just came across forced. When I went off the top of my head, it went better. Eventually, absolutely, it was a tremendous experience.

"But it was strange when the Imus stuff went down, because I had that relationship with Rutgers. When it happened, the day before—it was a Tuesday—I left work and started feeling rotten. I had a terrible stomach flu. The worst flu ever. And the next day, Sid [Rosenberg] was back on the air filling in for me and he was down in Florida. I didn't hear it because I was so out of it for two days and that's when he said it. I wasn't even there. It steamrolled.

"I was out of work the rest of the week with the flu and was in this strange position: in the middle between Rutgers, which I obviously had a great relationship with, and this guy who I worked for every day. I felt strange about going back to work. What he said, I thought was disgusting. And on Sunday night, before going back to WFAN, I was seriously contemplating not going to work."

But this is where Carlin began to push past the crisis. And he played it smart. Carlin spoke with the chief decision maker at WFAN, and then with Rutgers' representatives.

"Yeah, Mark Chernoff put me at ease about the whole thing, and so did [athletic director] Bob Mulcahy from Rutgers," Carlin recalled. "Bob called me and said, 'Hey, you're our guy. We know you weren't there. We know you'd never be a part of it. You have nothing to worry about.' I was just newly married at 34 and had just signed a contract earlier that year. I thought, *That's how this is going to go, huh?* So I went back to work and Imus was very gracious to me, saying he appreciated the fact here's a guy that works for [Rutgers] and came to support me. It was a strange dynamic for a few days."

The weeks that followed weren't much different. The aftermath of seeing a legend fired wasn't just going to pass. How would WFAN respond? How would the listeners react? Who the hell was going to replace him?

"I recall sitting in Mark Chernoff's office the day that Imus was let go," Spitz said, "and I was in stunned disbelief. We couldn't believe that it actually happened. So it was certainly a very difficult time at the station and Mark Chernoff, who deserves so much credit for WFAN's success, just went out and did it. No feeling sorry. No reminiscing. Nothing. We just moved on."

Indeed, Chernoff and Spitz hit the ground running. How they were going to do, what they were going to do, and who they were going to do it with, well, no one quite knew. But this was a station built on overcoming challenges, quieting critics, and smashing stumbling blocks.

What was another one, right?

"I wasn't sure what direction to go, and I thought to myself, *Do we replace Imus with someone who is like Imus? Or do we go something more sports?* We do sports most of the day, so maybe the morning show has to be more sports-oriented," Chernoff recalled.

"So I had Mike and Chris do shows in the morning. And we tried some other things but I said to myself 'Maybe this needs to be more sports.' Take this as a new opportunity, I thought.

"So, Boomer Esiason calls me one day and says 'Hey, I'd really like to be considered.' He had done some fill-in shows, and he was a great guest as the Jets quarterback. But I said, 'Really, Boomer? Really, you're going to get up at 4:00 in the morning?' He said, 'Oh yeah, no problem.' I said, 'Okay,' and I gave him a week of shows. I thought about it. In the end, I said to Boomer, 'Eh. It's okay, but it's not really what I was looking for.'"

Esiason wasn't alone in not piquing Chernoff's interest. Fox News Channel star Geraldo Rivera didn't, either. Nor did Lou Dobbs, at the time a CNN staple; Patrick and John McEnroe of professional tennis fame; MSNBC's Joe Scarborough; CNBC's Jim Cramer; and Monica Crowley, formerly of Westwood One radio.

In the end, he settled on a journeyman host from New Rochelle, New York, and a former four-time Pro Bowl quarterback from Long Island. It was a gut feeling, just something that felt right, albeit spontaneous.

"I talked with Chris Oliviero over at corporate, and we had chased after Craig Carton a few years before, and his name came up again. I was very interested in him," Chernoff said. "So, I wanted to approach Craig for WFAN, and it turns out, his contract was coming to an end, and I said to him, 'Hey, are you interested?' And he was very interested because he wanted to get out of the Jersey station he was at [WKXW FM 101.5]. He had been an intern here at FAN, he had been at WIP [AM 610 in Philadelphia], and he loved sports.

"So I said, 'Maybe I'd like to try you and Boomer Esiason, let's see if there's anything there.' So, I had them meet over at the old WNEW FM [102.7] studios. They chatted a little bit, I put them in a studio, and I said 'Here's four topics, mostly sports, let's see how you do.' And literally, not after five minutes—I was sitting with Chris Oliviero—I said 'That's my new morning show.' I said 'It's not going to be Imus, it's going to be different. It's going to be sports. But it's going to be fun, I think there's a chemistry there,' and that's how it became *the* show."

It was a move sure to be discussed. There's Esiason, who would have to break through the stereotypical theory that football players can't do much else than play football. And then there was Carton, a shock jock who was toiling in the Garden State. "That's your new morning show," people asked. "*You sure?*"

"Yep. A lot of radio is feel, and Mark felt it. He dug in and made the call," Spitz said. "He came to me after that audition and there was no hesitation. Mark has dealt with some of the biggest radio personalities of all time—the best—and he just knew this was it. Period."

Boomer & Carton ticked many of the boxes WFAN needed. The station, in the wake of Imus, knew it had go big, and had to be *different*. This was both.

In Esiason, you had the New York superstar athlete who rose to fame as a Cincinnati Bengals signal caller, but also played for the Jets and loved the New York sports landscape. In Carton, you had the outspoken one, a controversial but finely tuned broadcaster who knew how to stir debate. He wasn't perfect—Carton and WIP ran into trouble in Philadelphia with comments about former Flyers center Eric Lindros in 1997—but he was bold, brash, and wasn't afraid to break news.

You see, Carton developed relationships with many insiders. To this day on WFAN, you'll hear Carton break a story—as if he was a beat writer—when a team makes a move. He gets "in" with the right sources, and that added to his marketability. Whether or not Lindros, the Flyers captain, actually missed a game because he was hungover doesn't matter much now. It simply showed what Carton was all about.

He was confident in his ability. He trusted his relationships. And he wasn't afraid to take risks. Kind of like Chernoff.

"The idea was let's get the *best* show," Spitz said. "It's still very entertaining, like Imus, but different. It certainly included much more sports than Imus had, and fit better into the fabric of what the station was doing overall.

"It just worked from Day 1. And it only got better in Day 2. It was a monumental moment in the history of the radio station."

And with each new morning, Esiason and Carton continue to build a brand. Both New Yorkers who get the listenership, they each have their own schtick that they refuse to back away from. Nothing is out of bounds, and it all adds up to what's become a monster of a program.

"You're never really sure—even though there is a chemistry there—how a new show was going to do, but we took a chance. There really was a lot of emotion going through me for a long time there because of Imus," Chernoff said on April 24, 2013. "But I knew I had to move forward. I said, 'Let's go for it.' And you know what? Luckily, the guys clicked, the chemistry has been great, and it's been six years, which seems impossible it's been *that* long. They've held their own, they've been rated number one for men's 25-54—our target age demographic—and they've been able to do sports, lifestyle, politics, you name it.

"My M.O. has always been 'Everything we do, should emanate from the world of sports. But we can go a little bit farther because it's a morning show, and people want to be entertained.' They've done all of it."

Just ask one of the hosts who takes over for them at 10:00 AM.

"I think it was the best decision they ever made. You don't want to try to recreate Don Imus. He is a legend, no doubt. I'll admit: I was a kid. I didn't really listen to him that much because I wasn't into what he was talking about. Funny, now I'm into politics, so maybe I would have appreciated it a decade and a half ago. But Boomer and Carton are actually the perfect team," said Evan Roberts, who mans The Fan's midday with Joe Benigno.

"I've talked about *Mike and the Mad Dog* being the greatest team of all time. I stand by that. But Craig and Boomer are perfect because they mix with each other so well. Boomer is the athlete, the guy that is dignified, and Carton is hilarious and has crazy opinions. They're great for the station. It is a mix, sure. I don't think of them as a sports show but I don't think of them as not a sports show. They're in the middle...and that's original.

"It's definitely different for us in that we used to come on Monday mornings at 10:05, we were the first group to talk about sports. Now? Different story."

Being themselves, being true on the air, certainly helps. They don't try to hide who they are, and that works in radio because other hosts—and more importantly, the listeners—will call you out otherwise. As Benigno says, "there are a lot of frauds in this business." And that gets exposed over the long haul.

"You have to be ready for anything, you *have* to have thick skin," update anchor Jerry Recco said. "I learned right away that I was in the line of fire, that if you had a flaw, anything, they would latch onto it. My first time, I had a pimple on my forehead, and Craig turned it into one of the funniest segments in radio. It turned into *the joke* of the day. It was tough, but you get used to it, and then you learn to give it back to them."

It wasn't easy *for anyone* in the beginning. Not only was New York out there to conquer. There was the inner office, as well.

"The early days sucked because other than [evening host] Steve Somers and Mark Chernoff, nobody on the radio station believed that we'd be successful," Carton said. "So we kind of fought the fact that we were new, that obviously we were here to do a different kind of show and we were kind of viewed as outsiders when we first got here.

"So, we had to fight perception. And we always go back to the great quote we use a lot—*Do you even like sports?*—and we tried to convince people that A. We knew what we were doing; and B. The audience will flock to it if given the amount of time that we needed."

He was right.

"The morning hasn't missed a beat, and the ratings are even better now," Carlin said. "I credit Mark Chernoff with that because that was a Herculean task. Good luck with that. To be able to put those two together and see them work as well as they have, what a move."

MSG Network, a cable channel beamed into homes across the metropolitan area, agreed. In September 2010, the station began simulcasting *Boomer & Carton*, adding a whole new dimension. The studio is now dressed up in man-cave-like fashion for the cameras, and you see the many faces of Carton, as he traditionally rests his forearm on top of his microphone as if it's someone's shoulder. All in all, you get an up-close look at all the moving parts of the program—Recco, producers Al Dukes and Eddie Scozzare—and what makes it stand out.

"Well, we replaced Imus, one of the pillars of radio broadcasting," Carton said. "We knew we *had* to be different."

That's never been a problem.

"Craig had already been successful, and I used to listen to him a lot in Jersey, so it was never a thought in my mind that he couldn't adjust," Recco said. "I thought he was a brilliant radio guy and I always found his show funny and incredibly informative. What I've found since, is that he's one of the smartest people you'll meet. He can have a conversation about anything, he's very well read. And I honestly believe he can do a financial show. That's how intelligent he is."

He's not alone.

"You have the former athlete who knows his football and is a passionate hockey fan—loves his Rangers—and watches the NBA and the Knicks and is a big-time Met fan as well. He's a passionate guy, he's well-planted in the area, Long Island guy. You start with him," said Marc Malusis, an overnight host on WFAN. "When you look at Craig, he's an entertainer. He knows sports, obviously, too, but has a style that can ruffle your feathers. He can joke around and does a tremendous job of running the show, getting the best out of the callers.

"He may rub some people the wrong way but that's what a host is there to do. You don't want everyone to be vanilla all the time. It comes with the territory. Not everyone is going to love you. As long as they listen, that's all that matters. And he does that. Bottom line? They entertain, they inform, they've got passion. It's a tremendous combo."

One that continues to evolve, yet remains unpredictable. One day, they'll spend time on Boomer's recreational hockey team. The next, they'll start a movement to get Mets third baseman David Wright into the All-Star Game. In either case, they are sparking interest.

"We think back to Day 1 a lot, and we were happy. We thought it was extremely funny, and it was exactly what our individual personalities were all about," Esiason said. "I don't think we have had one bad day at work since. We both said the same thing at the start: 'Remember that we're on the same team. Remember that we are both going to have thick skin. And let's do it.'

"For me personally, I have loved it and I enjoy coming to work every single day. Because the whole thing has been totally unpredictable, totally spontaneous. It's a different show every morning, that's what makes it so much fun. We've never had one bad day together."

They disagree plenty, of course. But not on that topic.

"Those tryout shows that we did, they were the same show that we did today. We just got lucky. We start each show with the same idea. We don't take each other that seriously," Carton said. "We're not going to break down every inch of every single sport. But we're going to do our show for four and a half hours, and have fun, and Boom's right. We have not had a true cross word, on or off air. There have been no issues.

"There's never been a need for a 'Hey, we need to talk about this or that.' Boomer brings what he brings. I bring what I bring. And we got really lucky."

That's not lost on their WFAN teammates. They are both a part of the fabric of the station now, even though they were formed from an ugly situation.

"I thought Imus got hosed, to be honest with you, with that whole thing that went down, that forced him out," Benigno said of his former colleague who was snapped up by Citadel Media, which is now Cumulus Media Networks, a company that moved his show to the Fox Business Network. "But these guys, they're very good at what they do. There's no doubt about it. It's more entertainment than anything else; I don't look at them as being hardcore sports guys. Obviously, Boomer knows his football, knows hockey. But it's more from a player's perspective. That's always a little different than the fans' perspective.

"But I think as far as entertainment value, I think they're very good. I think Carton's a terrific talk show host. I don't think he's a big-time sports guy. But I do think he's a very good show host, and entertaining."

Esiason indeed milks the player perspective. Not a show goes by where he doesn't inject an experience and how it might relate. But people don't get sick of it. You have the shock jock on one side of the studio, and the jock jock on the other.

"I'm one of the guys around here who didn't play Strat-O-Matic Baseball when I was a kid," Esiason said. "I actually *played* the game."

Carton didn't, and it doesn't matter because he'll get on Esiason for leaning on that crutch too much, and Esiason will fire back that at least he has that crutch to work with. Fireworks often ensue, but it's all in good fun.

"When people ask about the show, it's the same thing," Esiason said. "I always get 'How do you work with *that* guy?' I respond the same way: 'Listen, this guy is the starter. He kicks it all off, he's great at it, and I just follow it up.'"

Their team certainly helps. Recco is an ideal fit, as he sits to Boomer's right, serving scores and soundbites with a kick. Dukes orchestrates playful copycat songs that would make Weird Al Yankovic proud, and Scozzare is the veteran calming influence that keeps the ship on course.

"The morning drive is a completely different animal from the afternoon drive, from the midday, overnights, whatever," Esiason said. "We have to be entertaining, informative, and have to be able to touch on a lot of things."

"We have an outline, and we discuss it, and though nothing is scripted, we do have an idea of where we want to go with things," Carton said. "We try to keep up with as much as possible."

"And it doesn't always have to be sports. It can be our personal lives. But it's good," Esiason said. "I do believe, in the mornings, when people are stuck in their cars, and they're going to work, many times they can be miserable. On Mondays, after your NFL team may have lost, or if you're a Knicks fan, and they lost the night before to the Miami Heat, to inject some humor in there, and to have some fun, and to actually act as if we love coming to work, I think it is appreciated by the morning drive audience.

"We're different from that standpoint. And I'm not a longtime radio guy like Chernoff and Craig is. But the fact of the matter is it's working."

Imus concurs. He doesn't listen often, but that doesn't mean he isn't aware of their impact.

"I've never actually listened. But I think they are fine. I may have heard snippets of them, but you know, they have done well, obviously," he said, quickly acknowledging that the strength of the station and the interest of the content certainly play into the equation. "But it's hard to lose there. It's just hard to lose on WFAN. It'd be difficult. You'd have to be really fucking awful.

"I mean sports is just a phenomenon. I mean one of the most popular people on my program now is Warner Wolf on sports. It's woven into the fabric of our society, and it galvanizes communities, so it's an important part of life on the planet."

Look no further than a former NFL star and his sidekick. They know what fuels the WFAN engine, and they are unafraid to try new things to keep the tank full.

In fact, on March 8, 2013, Esiason and Carton jumped into two courtside seats and called a Brooklyn Nets game. The station has always been open to trying different things to stand out. And when you do that on WFAN, people notice.

"It's huge for us," said Nets general manager Billy King, who also worked in the same role for the Philadelphia 76ers. "It's so much more than just a station, more than just a place our games are aired. It's WFAN, it means so much to the city, and we're fortunate. They're open to trying new ideas, we're open to trying new ideas, and I'll tell you something, it's not like that everywhere."

Enter Carton and Esiason, who did play-by-play and color commentary, respectively, on a big night in Brooklyn against the Washington Wizards. That's when Nets guard Deron Williams shook a shaky season, and had his grandest night with the recycled franchise. Williams set an NBA record for converting nine three-point shots in the first half. He hit two more in the second, and finished with 42 points while Brooklyn cruised, 95–78.

Big stage? Big win? Big result? Nothing fazed Boomer or Carton. Like Williams, they nailed it:

Carton: And now Williams breaks down into the front court. Williams, again, from three? And he...got it...again! Are you out of your mind?

Esiason: Eighteen points for Deron Williams, who is what I would say 'Feeling it, Craigy!'

Carton: Un-be-lieve-able start for Deron Williams! He has not missed a three-pointer yet! Six for six! Eighteen points! And the Nets lead...22–2...on the Nets Radio WFAN Broadcast Network!

Their calls were used as soundbites for days. And while a little out of practice in some spots, they let Williams do the acting, and they just talked along.

"I've always felt the players you enjoy watching on the field, often are the ones who look like they're having the best time. I think there's a real connection from player to fan when there's a level of purity to it," said Howie Rose, a WFAN original. "That explains *Boomer &*

Carton. If two guys on the air have *that* kind of chemistry, then we see them as having fun. That show is predicated on teasing each other and kidding around, but they do seem to like each other.

"That's what I find appealing. Even though they horse around, because they like each other, it draws me in. I'm a sucker for people who get along. I find the show quite enjoyable in that way."

He's not alone. Just ask one of those hosts Rose is talking about.

"I was exposed to this radio station a long time ago, on many levels," Esiason said. "As a New Yorker, as a contributor on *Imus*, I had a show with Mike and Chris during the football season for three straight years and I'll tell you—as Mark Chernoff is sitting right next to me as we talk—that I knew what I was getting into. I knew what The Fan was.

"What I didn't know is that I would enjoy it as much as I have. For me and Craig, it's all about being who we are, and being a part of a family, and then, taking those personalities, putting them together, and creating a fraternity house that people love listening to."

Pretty strong stuff from a former player who used to be best known for his 1988 NFL Most Valuable Player award, a quarterback who threw for 37,920 yards and was a two-time All-Pro.

Not to be outdone, of course, Carton had to top that reply…or at least try.

"Well," he said with a laugh. "We're pretty special. That's what we are."

11

Chris Gets Sirius

I thought the show was going to end on its own. I didn't think they were ever going to break up. Ever. Listen, I miss them together. I do. There's no question. But it is what it is and they both do very, very good shows on their own. I just don't know if they'll ever recapture the thing that they had together. Ever. —CHRIS CARLIN

CHRIS CARLIN OWES A GOOD PART of his industry experience to Mike Francesa and Chris Russo. As a playful producer for *Mike and the Mad Dog*, one who often took jabs from the two famous hosts in stride, and one who often laughed with the Dynamic Duo, even when he might not have wanted to, Carlin—while pushing buttons behind the glass and serving up New York's best sports talk show daily—was slowly carving out his own career.

Along the way, Francesa offered advice, and Russo opinion. Carlin took note of it all. He understood his place. He appreciated his opportunity. And he made the most of both.

Carlin is now a polished professional who has uncovered a bold brand, an unmistakable identity of his own. Stepping out of the shadow of *Mike and the Mad Dog*, he is now the radio play-by-play man for Rutgers football and basketball, the host of a sports opinion show on SportsNet New York, and the pre- and postgame frontman for New York Mets telecasts.

This comes after a jack-of-all-trades run at WFAN, in which he graduated to overnight host, to update man for *Imus in the Morning* and *Boomer & Carton*, and to New York Giants pre- and postgame host. In short, things sure have worked out for the large, jovial man that Russo and Francesa refer to as "The Continent."

But Carlin will never forget where he came from. And he will never forget the efficiency that Francesa and Russo used to deliver five and a half hours of a sports symphony. Which is why he was saddened and stunned when news broke that the two drive-time legends were to end their 19-year run. It was swift. It was sudden. And for many, it was a shocker.

"I can tell you that I, for one, didn't think it was ever going to happen," Carlin said. "The one time that I thought it might was when I was still producing the show. It was the summer of 2000, where they got into a massive fight. It was that Knicks-Pacers series [the NBA Eastern Conference Finals] that they got into a huge fight.

"We were supposed to go back to Indianapolis for Game 6 and something happened with our flights, where our flight was canceled and we would have to go and connect through Washington. And Mike decided, 'The heck with this. I'm not going.'

"So then, Chris wasn't happy about it. But we went back to the station, did the show there. You see, Mike was a big [Knicks coach Jeff] Van Gundy proponent and Dog was, too. I can't remember the specifics of what happened in the game but something happened where coaching clearly came through and the Knicks lost the game, and Dog, the next day, was all over Van Gundy. Well, they got into it *and just would not let up.*

"There's no doubt there was a little anger there from the day before. So, they got into it and basically did not want to speak to each other. They had a couple days before one of them went on vacation, and they wouldn't see each other all summer. I talked to them individually both at the time and they both said, 'I'm not doing it anymore with him. *I'm done. It's over.*' And that was in July. Mike got married later that summer and I don't know if it was July or August, but to Mike's new wife's credit, Roe, she saved it. I'm pretty sure that she said to him 'You have to invite Chris.' And he wasn't going to.

"In the end, he invited him and Dog came [to the wedding] and they kind of made up and that was the stepping stone to getting them back together. So, I credit Roe with that. She's an amazing woman. Not just from *that* standpoint; she's terrific with Mike. And I give her credit for saving the show.

"And after that moment, I just thought everything would always be the same. They'd be together, keep going. I never thought that [a breakup] was *really* going to happen."

Many agreed. But for others, a divorce was expected. Some felt, as their celebrity status reached new levels, that the Kaufman Astoria Studios just weren't big enough anymore. And on August 14, 2008, what many thought was the "inevitable," happened.

Russo, on vacation with his family, was released from his WFAN contract so that he could sign a five-year deal with Sirius Satellite Radio. He was given his own channel, where he could sculpt a new wave of sports talk, and earn $3 million a year. He joined Howard Stern, who previously left the tradition of regular radio, to help steer the ship of the business' new medium.

"It got to a point where after 19 years together, you could sense it. The arguments weren't more frequent, it was just that instead of hashing things out, they would let it slide. When that starts to happen, it's almost time to move on," said Ed Coleman, an original at WFAN.

"Both wanted to try something on their own. Chris got a great opportunity, which made it a no-brainer. Although he thought about it long and hard. I remember talking to him about it a lot—'What do you think I should do?' and blah, blah, blah. To me, it was simple. It was a lot of money for a long time. He was ready to leave and I think Mike was ready to be alone. I didn't necessarily see it coming years in advance, but as they got closer to splitting apart, it made sense."

As talk pulsed through the city louder than some of Russo's rants, the tabloids raced to get the story, callers flooded The Fan looking for details, and sports radio fans from all over wondered what happened, and what was next?

"That really was a tough time," said WFAN operations manager Mark Chernoff, who was not far removed from watching Don Imus be dismissed. Suddenly, he had lost two of his three on-air pillars. "In the past, Mike and Chris' contracts had never come up at the same time. But I guess, at that moment, because of the differing lengths of their contracts, within a few months, they were coming up. And at first, I thought both of them really wanted to stay. Mike very strongly wanted to stay. Chris had said he *wanted* to stay, but I guess he had other things in his head.

"Eventually, I finally got it that he just didn't want to be at the station anymore. For whatever his reasons were—personal, maybe he didn't want to be paired up anymore, or he just wanted to be out on his own—he went over to Sirius, and we were able to work something out. He was able to leave a little bit early. We all moved on."

With Russo out of town when the news broke, there was buzz, rumor, and innuendo, but not many facts. Finally, the next day, after a recorded, shortened opening featuring Russo's famous *"Aaaaaaaaaaaaaaaaaaand good afternoon everybody! How are you today? The* Mike and the Mad Dog *radio program,*" Francesa interrupted with the news:

"You know, and for 19 years—it was a week short of 19 years—that is how we welcomed New York to this program every day—or most days; sometimes not in the summer; sometimes there was a rare day here or there—but that was the sound that beckoned everybody to the start of the *Mike and the Mad Dog* radio program.

"As now you know, you learned last night that the *Mike and the Mad Dog* program would be no more, as Dog has decided to move on. And the response has been, to me, overwhelming. You know, we started this program on September 5, 1989. It was a shotgun wedding, as everyone may remember if you're old enough. It was almost a quickie divorce. We did not get along very well in the beginning. The show was considered to be a colossal misjudgment the first couple of weeks. Within nine months, it was the toast of the town.

"And fortunately, for Dog and myself, it has remained that for these many years. It has remained the show that has been at the top of the ratings, thankfully, for all of those years…because of you. And I know for many of you—and for me, and I know for Dog—this is a very sad occasion."

Later, Russo would call in, and after a few laughs to break the ice, offered up an explanation.

"Listen, I think that I need to address this lingering thought that I'm leaving because of you and I *not* getting along, and that is not the reason. I know you know that. I called you Wednesday night, I know you know that. And I think the audience is a little hesitant to think that maybe I'm leaving because you and I are fighting in the spring. That's not it.

"I'm 48, it's time for a little change for me, personally. I think this will both do us a little good. I think you'll do very well. I can tell you're challenged, looking forward to it. Whatever I decided....I just think I need a challenge in my life. A little something different.

"Now, I don't know how to handle what you just said there. Because you did a wonderful job. I feel, basically, the same way you do. I love that talk show. I love the fans, you love the fans, too. I'm going to miss that."

Emotions then began to take over.

"We did a wonderful show....I think you and I, with the big moment, were still as good as anybody. People don't realize how long five and a half hours is," Russo said. "I know Mike. He knows me better than Mike knows Roe, and better than I know [Russo's wife] Jeanne. That's the bottom line.

"Mike knew me before he knew Roe, before he had three kids. I knew Mike before I had four kids, and before I knew my wife, so ...." Russo paused, took a deep breath, exhaled, and tried to fight back tears to no avail. They came in bunches, and they were intertwined with his words. "It wasn't an easy call. I'm gonna miss that show."

The back and forth, with the pomp and circumstance, was great radio. Heartfelt. Entertaining. Memorable. But with one host in studio and on television thanks to the YES Network, and another on the phone from his vacation home, it was not the kind of an ending this show deserved.

"I thought FAN would let me stay around for a couple days, to do a good-bye thing, especially do that show at Bar A," Russo recalled. Bar Anticipation is a legendary Jersey Shore establishment in Lake Como, New Jersey, where Francesa and Russo traditionally held an end-of-summer show, complete with sports and musical guests. It was a lookback at what they had missed during vacation, and a lookahead to the busy fall, played out in front of several hundred fans with the glistening sun and the Atlantic Ocean as a backdrop.

"They didn't want to do that which I understand. I didn't understand at the time but I can understand now. That's why that last show was sort of a...it was tough."

And just like that, *Mike and the Mad Dog* was through. The show that helped brand a station, a staple that New York sports fans turned to for parts of three decades...washed away on a summer's night.

"You know, it wasn't easy. You get used to doing a show in a certain way. We did it that way for 20 years," said Francesa, who took the timeslot solo. "In the beginning, people wanted to reminiscence a lot. I understand that, but I thought it was important to move forward. I have always paid complete homage to *Mike and the Mad Dog*. It was a brilliant show. Remarkable. Legendary. Then we closed the door.

"I can't say I think about it very much now in my day-to-day. His show is different than mine in approach. My show is every bit as intense—maybe even more intense—than it was with Dog. It's fast moving. And I think the fans, they move on. That's one thing I realized. The audience doesn't stand pat. It goes forward. The wheel keeps turning.

"I always bring it back to when I was a kid and [former late night television host] Johnny Carson left, I said 'No one can replace Johnny Carson.' Well, they moved on. They didn't sit there every night and say 'Where's Johnny?' So, as performers, we have to move on. And that's what I tried to do. I really didn't try to give it *that* much thought."

But there was a mourning period. This was a story that broke the barriers of the New York sports media almost instantaneously. For a local show, it became a national phenomenon.

"It was very sad," said Marc Malusis, a former producer for *Mike and the Mad Dog*. "I remember talking to Chris that night and he said 'I just wanted to try something different,' and I said 'All right,' as long as he was happy and excited about the opportunity. For the sports fans in this area, they were *the best* on radio. No one will do it better. There's no show that will have the impact that they did because they broke the ground. They set the road.

"They were the first [sports] radio show to be on TV. Now, you have everyone on ESPN on TV, and *Boomer & Carton* are on MSG [Network] and Mike is still on YES. They did it first in the sports radio medium. They set the tone as to how to do it, how to do it the best, how to entertain, how to be knowledgeable, how to do the tough-hitting interview. The combination of Chris Russo and Mike Francesa...there will never be another combo that will be better."

Which made the decision so difficult. Personal differences aside, there still would have been plenty of positives had Russo stayed.

"I probably should have done a better job with Mike. To leave after 19 years with your partner? It's a very tricky situation, how to handle that. There's no handbook that tells you how to do it. I probably should have handled it a little differently," Russo said.

"I wouldn't have gone if they didn't give me a channel. I just felt—48 years of age—it was an opportunity that was not going to come again. Mike is a little older than me. He's a little more New York than I am. He likes the Yankees and Giants, and I don't like all the New York teams. So Mike wouldn't have taken that chance and I don't blame him. I was willing to give it a shot. Mike and I had done so well for so long. The money was not going to be a problem. It was going to be worth a shot for five years to see if it could work. If it didn't, fine, I'm still going to get paid. So from a monetary aspect, it really wasn't any risk.

"But it was a risk. Of course. A lot of people thought I was crazy. A lot of people understood. [But] I should have communicated with him better. I'm not so much concerned with the rest of the management of the station. They changed. I was more concerned about Mike. As far as making the decision, and Sirius offers you a channel—do what you want; do your own brand; make your own hires and fires—I think you have to be crazy not to do it. So I did.

"I wouldn't have gone to ESPN. I wasn't going to 1050 [AM New York, the chief competition of WFAN]. I just felt it was the right opportunity to take a swing at it."

Sirius indeed presented a new challenge for Russo, a tougher task, but he had autonomy to build his empire. That is a rarity in radio, in life for that matter. Mad Dog Radio was the name of the channel and it was much more than just an afternoon program. There was a morning show, a midday spot, and evening slot to all fill. Producers, update anchors, the list goes on. Russo was more than just a host. He was the CEO.

"I probably didn't know," Russo said, "how hard this job was before I took it."

Mad Dog Unleashed is not *Mike and the Mad Dog*. But you still get the effervescent, enthusiastic Russo, who is still one of a kind regardless of the medium. He's still loud with his laughs, and proud with his position. He still repeats many of his same thoughts, and he will never be a language pro, especially when it comes to formal names.

"Chris is Chris. He's a passionate sports fan. He's not going to pronounce everything correctly but that's part of his charm. He knows who he talks about. He knows what he talks about. He knows history, and has an opinion on everything. The passion is always there. And you get that on satellite radio," Malusis said.

"But it's just different and Chris will admit it. I'm not saying the shows aren't good, they are good. They're still great broadcasters, Marconi [Award] winners. It's just a different dynamic. I think Chris does a great job and I think Mike, obviously, has done a fantastic job."

Russo's timeslot shifted one hour on Sirius, running from 2:00 PM to 7:00 PM, rather than the 1:00 PM–to–6:30 PM spot that Francesa continued with. He still uses his patented

"Aaaaaaaaaaaaaaaaaaaand good afternoon everybody!" open, but *Mad Dog Unleashed* also features "Radio Nowhere," a 2007 selection from Russo's favorite musician, Bruce Springsteen.

"I have missed the give and take with Mike more than I thought. I have missed the give and take with New York more than I thought. There are positives here, too. I love the flexibility. I'm sure Mike does as well. I love the content. I can do San Francisco Giants baseball or Australian Open tennis to my heart's content," Russo said. "I don't like to be bogged down as much with the drudgery of breaking down [New York Jets coach] Rex Ryan's tattoo. So from a radio perspective, it's really freedom.

"Mike has freedom as well, because Mike doesn't have to worry about a partner. One of the things with me leaving that has really gone under the radar—and I've thought about it a lot—is the fact that I get bored sometimes breaking down the Yankee lineup. I would have gotten bored talking about [former New York Jets quarterback] Tim Tebow. So the idea I could go somewhere and not have to be tied down was appealing. I'm not a Yankee fan. I'm not a Met fan. I'm not a Knick fan. Those chains are off me.

"If I want to break down the '73 Sugar Bowl—Notre Dame and Alabama—I can do it. Of course, I have the time to do it because there's no commercials. So, you put all that together from a flexibility and content standpoint, you can't beat the job. There are some negatives. But from that standpoint, it's as good as it gets."

A prevailing thought about satellite when it launched—and especially when Stern joined—was that it would break rules regular radio couldn't. On satellite, you could be 'R' rated. But *Mad Dog Unleashed* doesn't drive down that road. The nighttime host on Russo's station, Dino Costa, authors a headline-grabbing show, equipped perfectly for satellite, in which callers traditionally let loose and Costa often offers up no-holds-barred commentary. It makes the most of the platform.

But on Russo's show, it's very rare that he pushes that envelope. He's 'PG-13', at best, and often brings up the youth sports that his children play on the air.

"That's something new, for sure," said Sweeny Murti, WFAN's Yankees beat reporter. "You have to remember when Mike and Chris were together, for a long time, they didn't have children. Now, that's a part of the equation, he pulls it off well, and that's Chris. Keep your listeners entertained, and he always has.

"I remember down at spring training, and I was in a rental car that had satellite. I was driving across Florida, had plenty of time, and I listened to Chris talk about [Russo's son] Timmy's team...*all day*. He got everyone in the act, his producers, the update guy, and then the callers took over, and it became a big discussion on youth sports. It was entertaining radio. Totally Chris."

Other times, it's Russo being Russo, just how New York remembers him. He still predicts games. He still rants and raves about his San Francisco Giants. He still engages the caller to get the absolute best out of two minutes. And he still, as Malusis put it best, "breaks balls."

"I'm friends with Chris. I hope to always be friends with Chris," said Jody McDonald, a WFAN original. "When you meet someone who has never met any of the WFAN people, usually they feel a need to ask about Chris. '*What is Chris Russo really like?*'

"My answer is always 'Chris Russo is exactly like what he is on the air.' He comes into the station with a big smile on his face, comes up and gives you an awkward hug and slaps you on the rear end. But that's Chris. And he screams and yells and is always up, ready to argue, ready to debate. It doesn't matter whether it's on the air, or out in the newsroom before the show, or out after a charity basketball game in the bar having a cocktail, that's Chris.

"Some people have their on-air persona and their off-air persona. Chris' persona is pretty much 24/7. That's what I like most about Chris, was that he was just genuine. He handles his life and his business the same. Once you got used to it, he could be a guy who was a lot of fun to hang around with."

He certainly has fun with his team at what is now SiriusXM. With less commercial time, he allows his crewmen opportunities to jump on the mic. Of course, that usually means Russo is going to take a few jabs, but that's nothing new.

"That's him. But it's in good fun," said Kevin Burkhardt, a former update man on WFAN. "I have to say, he was good to me from the beginning. At that place, I don't know if there was competition, but it just always felt like you were a Chris guy or you were a Mike guy. You know what, I was neither. I was treated well by both, but Chris was the guy that I went on with first.

"Chris says he quote *discovered* me, though [former WFAN program director] Eric Spitz will debate that one. Chris always made me relax, made me laugh, treated me great. 'Hey, where ya from? Tell me about ya.' He brought me on the air and made me part of the show that first day. Took a few shots at me, of course. But he didn't make me feel like an outsider. Didn't make me feel like some freelance guy coming in nervous as heck. I'll never forget that.

"The next Friday, after my debut, when I was on *Mike and the Mad Dog*, Chris made a big thing about me. I came in and did the update, and Marc Malusis was producing. You know how Chris always loves to tweak. After the update, he said, 'Hey Mikey, this Burkhardt, he's got a good voice, huh?'

"Of course, it started a whole thing that Malusis couldn't get any gigs and this Burkhardt guy was. But it was all a joke, and Chris was a guy you'd go in and joke with."

Burkhardt's experiences mirror those of Steve Torre's, the program director at Mad Dog Radio, who gives updates on *Mad Dog Unleashed*, makes predictions with Russo, and is very much part of the fabric of the show. He's also a Russo target quite often, and he's unafraid to fire back. Whether it's a debate about the Yankees bullpen, or their sons' youth baseball experiences from the past weekend, there's a bond there.

"You have to remember now, that the dynamics of Sirius, just from a facility standpoint are a lot different. Everyone in Sirius is in one studio. It's half the size of Mike's, even less than that. So, Torre and my guys are in with me. The four of us are basically in a box with four microphones. It is not your normal radio studio where there's a big partition between you and your engineer," Russo said. "It's a negative and a positive. The negative is you hear everyone's business, but the positive is it does give you an opportunity to try to get them involved a little bit. You almost have to.

"I'm probably a little hard on Torre. A little harder than I should be. But sometimes you need that foil. That's where I miss Mike. And that's where Mike and I, that's where the both of us miss each other. Because Mike knew that, after 19 years, he had an equal with me. I knew with Mike, I could throw anything at him and he could handle that. I don't have that right now, and that's hard.

"And there's nobody that I am going to get that is going to be able to fill the Mike role because they can't do it as well. And there's nobody that Mike is going to get that is going to fill the Chris role because he can't find anybody as good as me, either. So as a result, we lost our right arm, and you have to compensate for that. It's not a total loss, but it is a loss. And I bet you Mike would agree. It can be very tricky."

But five years at SiriusXM has helped. It is a grind, no question, and it's every bit the challenge that Russo thought it'd be when he altered sports radio with his decision in 2008.

"I love Francesa and Russo. Of course. And I thought Mike and Chris were great together. I do not think they're great individually *at all*. But I like both of them personally, they both were tremendously loyal to me when I got fired," Imus said, as he struck hard and fast in a memorable interview that seemingly ran through all of New York radio. "They unto themselves was just a great radio program. It was just enormously entertaining.

"But, you know, the whole ego thing got in the way, and Mike's got an enormous ego, as you know. Individually, there is not much there. That's my opinion only, as a listener. That is not a professional analysis. It's not difficult to take phone calls from idiots and talk sports, it's just not.

"But I love Chris. I had him on this morning."

Support or not, it's tough to stay ultra-relevant when you work for an outlet that many still don't subscribe to.

"I don't have Sirius at the station," said Russ Salzberg, sports anchor on WWOR TV Channel 9 in New York. "So, I'm really not listening to Chris."

He's not alone.

"I've never heard him since he left," said Steve Somers, the evening host on WFAN. "Not once."

Either way, Russo pushes forward, striving to be better. He leaves his house in New Canaan, Connecticut, boards a train for Manhattan, waltzes into that box of a studio and again becomes Mad Dog. He has the daily opportunity to make great sports radio, as he has his whole career. But it's just...

"Different, no question," Chernoff said. "When you're on in New York, and you have an audience of a million and a half or so people, versus whatever he has on satellite—and then you consider it's a national show versus local—it's a different deal. I think for Chris, to be able to talk about whatever he wants to talk about, when he wanted to, he has that leeway. When you're on in New York, you have to talk about what is going on in New York. That doesn't mean you can't tend to some of the other national topics, and our listeners know that. But in the end, it's New York.

"He likes national angles. We all used to kid him about the San Francisco Giants, but he now has that bigger picture to talk about that. But yeah, I listen and have listened to him there. Dog is Dog. He can be funny, and he can be serious when he wants to. And I just think that his array of topics can be a lot larger over there, and it's just something that wouldn't play well on this radio station on a regular basis.

"So I assume he's happy, and he seems to be reasonably happy. I don't think he gets the kind of phone calls that we generate here at WFAN, so maybe there's longer monologues. But in general, he's been happy over there."

Happy but honest as well. Russo knows his daily roadblocks. He's unafraid to admit them. And he's constantly thinking of ways to tackle them, critics and all.

"Now, I think it's a little harder for me than it would be for Mike because there's no local team here, and Mike can always go back to Jets or Giants. I can't necessarily do that, and I have more time to work with," Russo said. "So, as a result, Mike—he knows he can break at 2:17; he can break at 2:30. I've got to be smart how I use those breaks."

As Russo wound down that response, he paused to reflect, not unlike the open of the final *Mike and the Mad Dog* program. He took a breath, collected his final thought, exhaled, and reminisced one last time.

"There's a lot of Mike I miss, trust me," he said. "A lot of Mike I miss."

When Francesa learned of that commentary, he paused, scanned two decades, and summed up a show, a proud pairing, that will never be forgotten.

"From a personal standpoint, we had a great time together. We had a wonderful 20 years. I wouldn't trade one day of it," he said. "We built a great show. We built a legacy, there's no question.

"And we built a station."

12

Just Mike and a Mic

I listen. I watch. You want to know what's going on in New York, what people are talking about, he's still the place to go to. That hasn't changed. Probably not going to change. I'm watching Mike right now. —DAVE SIMS

MIKE FRANCESA PICKED UP A RINGING CELL PHONE in his car at 6:31 PM on March 19, 2013, just a few minutes after he wrapped up another weekday afternoon sports talk show in New York City. After a few months of phone tag, a connection was made.

"Yes, this is Mike."

"Michael, Tim Sullivan here. Do you have a few minutes to chat?"

"Tim, right, the book. Right. Is this something we can do right now? Something I can do from the car?"

"Absolutely, Mike. Whatever works. I'm ready."

"Okay, let's go then. Let's do it."

Francesa was on his way out of Manhattan and headed toward his Long Island home, where his wife, Roe, and three children awaited. It was your normal day at WFAN for this sports media mogul. It was a Tuesday in March, so the NCAA tournament dominated. A little spring training was added to the mix, and some five hours later, his day was done.

As Francesa began to answer questions, he gazed outside of his window to see the city, *his city*, as darkness fell. He wasn't driving—that was left to Julio, his "driver," a New York City auxiliary police officer who goes pretty much wherever Francesa goes—so he truly had time to share some vivid memories as the bright lights of the big city swooshed on by. No need to worry about the traffic or the lane closures on this night, folks. Julio would take care of all of that.

Instead, Francesa scanned his encyclopedic memory bank, and spoke with confidence, pride, and devotion. This is a man, after all, who has shared the city radio spotlight with many across a decades-long career. But as the year in sports, 2013, truly kicked into gear, there was no doubt who this town belonged to.

"Frankly, I am where I always wanted to be," Francesa said. "I look at the station in chapters. The early success of FAN, a chapter, the adoring years of *Mike and the Mad Dog*, a chapter, and then the next chapter which was after Dog left. I had to prove all over again that FAN could have that continued success and I was the one to deal with that. That was on my shoulders.

"Don Imus left and Dog right after him. Frankly, when that all happened, it really put me in a different position. We had incredible success, and then they were gone, and then I wanted to be able to take it to a different place, and be able to have that next story, that next generation with FAN. I've been able to do that. That's something I'm proud of."

Francesa, with Chris "Mad Dog" Russo, built a sports radio empire at WFAN. *Mike and the Mad Dog* became the signature show for the station, and the standard by which all sports talk shows would be judged nationwide.

But it ended on August 14, 2008. Russo left the station for satellite radio and his own channel. After many good times—and plenty of bad—en route to carving out two of the most memorable careers in radio, the Dynamic Duo was suddenly over on a hot summer's day.

"A lot of opportunities were presented to me through the years," Francesa said. "He had opportunities presented to him. But we were fortunate that we stayed together and we saw this thing through. When it was time for him to move on, though, it was time."

Not long after the station's management wrestled with the Don Imus–Rutgers controversy—and the process of replacing one radio icon—they had to replace another.

"Over the years, they certainly had their moments of not getting along and they'd be the first to say it," former WFAN program director Eric Spitz said. "But you always felt ultimately they would figure it out and would stay together. Two high-personality, high-profile guys, there are always going to be issues, but when they sat down in the studio, it always just seemed right. When that didn't happen anymore, it just seemed wrong."

So did the alternatives. The notion of bringing someone in from the outside. The possibility of promoting someone from the inside. Nothing seemed right.

"They were thinking about getting a partner. As a matter of fact, I talked to [WFAN operations manager] Mark Chernoff about the possibility of me being *that* guy," said Jody McDonald, an original at WFAN. "But they wanted whoever they were thinking about to come in and do shows with him. Trial runs, call them what you want, practice shows. And I was working for ESPN New York. And they were paying me pretty good money. There's a natural competition between the two stations, and ESPN New York was not going to allow me to go over for a test."

Sid Rosenberg figured to be in the mix as well. An emotional roller coaster who has battled addiction, Rosenberg knew New York sports, knew how to captivate an audience, and could be as loud as Russo. But that didn't happen, either.

"Mike has been there for me. Mike tried desperately—he'll deny this to the day he dies, I don't care—he tried desperately, had three secret meetings with CBS early in the morning, to get me the job when Russo left," Rosenberg said. "And CBS shot him down every single time."

Max Kellerman, a boxing specialist who rose to sports talk show status on ESPN New York, was another name, along with *ESPN The Magazine*'s Bill Simmons, a witty words wizard who was breaking free of his print background. There were others, but no one stood out. Maybe that was just because there was only one Russo. And, for that matter, just *one* Francesa.

"I knew there was a lot to be responsible for. I also knew that a lot of people were going to view me based on what happened in these next five years," Francesa said. "It was not going to be what I had accomplished with Dog. It was going to be now what I did without him. I knew I could do it. But how I was going to approach it was the important part. I thought of different things."

So, too, did Chernoff and Spitz. And after some discussion, the notion of replacing Russo seemed silly, and more importantly, impossible.

"As a collective, they decided that Mike would go with it solo. What Chris was and what Chris brought to the table was just too much to replace. So, they decided to forget it," McDonald said. "I knew Mike was good enough to do it by himself. I think most people did. The question was *how* would he do it."

Francesa spent a lot of time on that. What to do here. What not to do there.

"But after about after a month—thinking about where I wanted to take this—I stopped," he said. "I just remember one day I went in and I said, 'I'm not thinking about anything else anymore. There's no more debate about anything. I'm going back to being me.' From that moment, after thinking of a million different things, I just decided to be myself."

He signed a new five-year contract, and just like that, *Mad Dog Unleashed* was on Sirius, and *Mike'd Up* was on WFAN.

"I never looked back after that," Francesa said. "Thankfully we've been very successful. It was a challenging time, there's no question. I have no doubts that *Mike and the Mad Dog* would have been adoring. I don't know exactly where we would have been today. It's very hard to say. You don't know when a show has run its course. It's unpredictable. Dog and I were able to consistently get the numbers for 20 years. And I've been able to get them, consistently, since he left.

"If Dog was still here? If I had put someone else on the show with me? Who knows what would have happened. All I can judge it by is how it turned out. And fortunately, it turned out great, so I'm very lucky."

Mike'd Up, now named *Mike's On*, evolves daily. The Super Bowl trivia contest is much more subdued. The update men still stay in the studio sometimes to share a laugh, just not as loud a one. And the phone lines are still jammed.

"Mike has had bang-up ratings, but we certainly miss Chris. *Mike and the Mad Dog* was an iconic show and there's been nothing like it. A lot of people have tried to do teams, and be like them, but they were the standard, they led the way, they were the first, they were the best," Chernoff said.

"And in the few times that they've been on the air together since, that chemistry is always there, even if it's 15 minutes, a half hour. There's still that twinge of missing that on our end, no question, at the radio station.

"Mike—like I did—had trepidations at first. Should he have a partner, should he do it alone. And then it just came to me that if he was going to work with anybody at all, it was going to be Dog."

Mike's On has its critics—especially on social media where a younger WFAN generation vents—but the show fits the host, the station, and for the most part, the audience. That doesn't mean, though, that there aren't some bad apples out there.

"I can be very hard on callers. I can be challenging to them, give them a hard time. My theory has always been that I treat the caller completely different than the audience. I have nothing but complete adoration for the audience. If you didn't have that for your audience, you'd be pretty stupid because that's the reason for your success," Francesa said.

"But I've always differentiated the audience and the caller. The caller is 1 percent. Most people never call. The caller, to me, when he enters your venue, he is performing. He has decided he wants to be part of the show. With that comes a responsibility. I want him to step up, make his point, and then defend and debate it. That's what makes good radio.

"You can't react to all points the same. It could be a good point, bad point, terrible point, stupid point, wonderful point, aggressive point, obnoxious point, whatever it may be, I'm going to react differently. If you react to all of them the same, it's not real. I try to be real. If a caller annoys me, I'll let you know he annoys me. If the caller amuses me, I'll let you know he amuses me, okay? I may be short and contentious sometimes, but I'm being real.

"The caller who says 'Oh, you have no respect for the audience...' No, no, no. I'm treating the caller as part of the program, okay? He has entered the venue. He wants to perform. And I want to treat them like I have expectations for them. To come on my show, I want them to raise their game. If they're not, then don't call. You can listen, don't call. You call, you are taking it to the next level.

"Everyone should have their own way. My relationship with callers is completely different than anyone else on the station and that's positive. What makes a good talk show host is if you can entertain, if you can educate, and can you can be unique? Can you bring your own special point of view? And I've been very fortunate in that people want to hear my take. They haven't gotten tired of that, thank God. To me, that is my gift.

"It's opinionated and it's very unique. Because it's mine. It's no one else's. And that's why I think it has stood the test of time."

And since another WFAN contract was signed by Francesa a month after this interview, it's obvious management agrees.

"It's not a knock on Dog, but most of the time he's talking about something I don't care about, you know what I mean?" asked Evan Roberts, a WFAN midday host. "I still like hearing about New York sports and the one thing about The Fan—which is why I think we'll always be around—is that New Yorkers care about New York. We care about what's going on around here. And I guess I fall into that same category, so if I flip over to Dog and he's talking about the Kansas City Chiefs, no offense, I don't really care that much.

"So I think that's probably why Mike's much easier to listen to because I want to hear about what's going on around here. I know, I know, those arrogant New Yorkers, we don't care about anything else."

But while New York is the prime focus, one thing Francesa—and Russo—excels at is stepping out of the box to expound on real life. It's unfortunate when it has to happen, but when a day takes on a horrific tone in the real world, Francesa has perfected the art of dropping sports to focus on what truly matters. And it doesn't go unnoticed.

"To a lot of people, Mike doesn't have a warm side. But he's always shown that to me. I've always felt like Mike's been in my corner. I'll go to bat for the guy. He's a brilliant sports mind," said Steve Levy, a former update man at WFAN and now a *SportsCenter* anchor on ESPN. "I have never seen anyone, to this day, who can have an immediate, breaking, big story and come out with the right thing to say shortly afterward better than Mike.

"There are a lot of people who are really smart hours after a big story breaks because they've had time to form opinions and process the information. '*Which way do we want to go on this?*' When you have time, those answers are easy to formulate. But when stories break, not so much, and Mike Francesa is the first to have what I think is a very strong and intelligent opinion. I really believe he is the best at that."

And as Francesa has aged and experienced more of the important things in life—marriage, children, health—he translates that across WFAN's air. Doesn't have to be sports. Doesn't have to be New York.

On December 14, 2012, 20 children and six adults lost their lives in a mass murder at Sandy Hook Elementary School in Newtown, Connecticut. It was a tragedy so enormous, so horrifying, it gripped a nation for months. In the hours after the shooting, after 20-year-old Adam Lanza committed these unthinkable acts before committing suicide, Francesa watched the news coverage from his studio. Even though as a parent, as an American, he was thinking of the victims, and perhaps even his own family back at home, he journeyed on.

As he took calls from Connecticut natives, and mixed in some updates from the television and wire reports, you could see the emotion building up. It was truly stirring radio from a man known more for his memories of Mickey Mantle and Lawrence Taylor.

He spoke in quick sentences, with long pauses, almost as if to honor those who were lost. And as he gazed into the YES Network cameras, his eyes appeared to well up.

"Think about it...He devastated a community...How many families tonight are going to be without...one of their children?...Or how many families tonight are going to be without...one of their parents?...Not to mention the kids who were traumatized in that school, who did nothing wrong today, except got up this morning and went to kindergarten."

Francesa adjusted his glasses, covered his mouth, and just shook his head as his thoughts began to race. His studio was decked out in Christmas gear for the YES cameras, but this was no holiday.

"Here's an unfulfilled 20-year-old who strikes out in his rage at his parents. Except he does it in a premeditated way where he will leave his mark."

Again taking a pause, again shaking his head at the horror, Francesa—capturing a story like Levy remembers—turned to his phone board, and got back to work…seamlessly.

"John in Bridgeport. What's up, John…"

Over on satellite, Russo, a Connecticut resident, was doing the same. It was almost as if, for one day, Francesa and Russo were together again because the content came from the heart so effortlessly. Two different hosts. Two different shows. Two different forms of radio. But through it all, there was unforgettable symmetry.

"Can you imagine being one of those parents tonight," Russo asked, stopping to take a breath. "Can…you…freakin'…imagine?"

"It's very difficult to focus. That was one of the hardest days I've ever had to work, Newtown. A very tricky day," Russo said. "Mike will speak to this as well—and I think 30 years in radio teaches you how to do it—but you have to trust your instincts.

"We both have kids. I don't live too far from Newtown. Mike has three little kids the same age as the kids who got shot. You put that into the equation. I don't think Mike ever did own a gun. I certainly don't own guns. That was a dramatic sequence when you're on right away, and the show's got to go on.

"You've got to do something. You can't break down. You're on for five hours. You stay on it. I did Newtown the next three or four days the following week. It's almost imperative that at times where there is a crisis, you do it.

"A lot of people that I've run into mentioned that day to me, they thought I did a good job with Newtown, and I'm sure Mike was the same. No question, it hit home for us."

Ability takes over in those instances, and boatloads of experience help Francesa to navigate those waters. But on September 10, 2012, by his own admission, he strayed off course and learned a lesson in just how stories can take off in this new media age.

While interviewing Yankees beat reporter Sweeny Murti, as the two discussed the fading Boston Red Sox, Francesa's head began to slump, his eyes closed, and he began to fade himself. His head drifted toward the lavender, short-sleeved golf shirt he wore that day, and he appeared to fall asleep while Murti's response reverberated into his black stethoscope-like headphones.

Eventually, he caught himself, perked up, stared right into the YES cameras with stunned eyes now wide open, asked his producers something that did not go on air, and went about the business of the interview.

"All right, we're talking with Sweeny, obviously, as we get ready for a trip to Boston, and then back home for a weekend against Tampa..."

"It was a Monday and the Yankees were going to start a series in Boston the next day," Murti recalled. "What I really remember—as we were talking about past Red Sox–Yankees series—was I was talking to him while looking up some history. I was looking for a specific stat. And I couldn't find it.

"So, I was stalling him, I was reeling a little bit. I knew I was doing it. I just kept stalling until I could find it, and never did. But as I do so many times, I talked around it, which is why my answer dragged on. But all along, you have to remember, I was on the phone, he was on the radio, and I wasn't watching on TV...so I had no idea what he was doing in front of the camera."

Francesa's recovery did little to stop the masses from thinking he fell asleep on the air. And that notion, complete with clips from YES, went viral on the Internet.

"It was posted online Tuesday, but not many people did anything with it," Murti said. "Wednesday is when it *really* blew up.

"Suddenly, I started getting texts and tweets, and I was like 'Oh, crap.' My first reaction was that this doesn't make me look any good either. I'm talking...and a man fell asleep! Are you kidding me?

"But the more it went on, the more it was Mike, he's the big personality, he's the guy that people take offense to, and so he took the brunt. It's his show, even though I was the guy talking, I was the guy who put a man to sleep!

"Once it took off, though, it *really* took off. I had players come up to me. I had one text me. And my response at the time was, 'Hey, you know me, I'm much more boring in person.' I had to find a way to laugh it off. I really didn't know what to say because Mike didn't address it until the following day."

Now, there are millions of views on YouTube of the incident. Twitter posts by the thousands featured screen shots, and plenty of commentary. Indeed, it was a lesson in how fast damage can be done to one's reputation.

So, on September 13, after being urged to do so by his wife, Francesa, 58 at the time, opened his show with an explanation of the events. He did not admit to falling asleep, only that he was tired from not getting much sleep the night before.

"I wasn't going to address this, and often I don't like wasting your time and my time with nonsense. But since it has become a story—it was in the paper today. You know, and the only reason I'm doing this today is because my wife won't talk to me until I do it.

Umm. Sunday, when we opened the season up, with the *NFL Now*, I did what I usually do. I got up at 6:00 Sunday morning, came in here and did the *NFL Now*. I went home, watched football, and by the time my day's over, it's 1:00 in the morning.

"And then, as happens, one of your kids gets sick. And that happened. One of my sons suffers from asthma, Jack, and recently, as the weather changes, he has some exercise-induced asthma. And I didn't get to sleep Sunday night, so that happens as a parent. Luckily, I have healthy kids, and sometimes it happens.

"Well, I came in, and I hadn't slept all night. I was dragging during the show which led to me closing my eyes during a Sweeny Murti interview, and causing this hurrah which none of us here knew about until yesterday, because people are now accusing me of being asleep during Sweeny, because I closed my eyes during the interview...which I shouldn't have done. And I was exhausted.

"But I can tell you this. I did close my eyes during the Sweeny interview and that was on TV and it's become this bone of contention because I guess everything we do on this show does. But I promise you, I was never asleep. I promise you. I promise you I won't come in without sleeping because my wife said I can't do that anymore."

His show went on. But the story wasn't forgotten. As the weeks wore on, he'd receive more prank calls about it. He took them in stride, laughing some off, scoffing at others.

"And as we talk about it now," Murti said, "honestly, I can tell you that I have never spoken to Mike about this. My mind-set, going into any talk we might have, was I was willing to fall on my sword here and make a joke of it, and apologize for rambling and being boring. I was ready for all of that. But we never talked about it. We did a regular Yankees segment that Thursday, it didn't come up, and that was it! He didn't bring it up, and I know I wasn't going to bring it up."

But everyone else did.

"It's a tough spot. He got burned because it's on YES. Whether Mike nodded off, didn't nod off, whether he fell asleep or not—and I know Mike well—it looked like he did," Russo said. "And so as a result, if it looks like he did, it's a tricky situation for Mike to come back from. Mike's probably a little embarrassed by that. Sometimes it's not easy to poke fun at yourself. If Mike poked fun, maybe this would've been different. But Mike's prideful. He's been very successful. He won a Marconi [Award] four days later, let's not forget that.

"It wasn't *that* dramatic. I haven't spoken to him so this is just me. But Mike was a little hurt by that. Mike was hurt that he had been on the air for 25 years and everybody now is going to think of Mike as the guy who fell asleep. Whether he did or not, that's the perception. I think down deep that bothers Mike. And you can't blame him. I understand.

"He's had a hell of a career. I think as a result, when he saw what a big story it was, he lashed out. He may have been a little better off pulling it back just a touch, poke tons of fun and it would have been a different situation. But I understand. I would have done the same thing. You get annoyed. You get frustrated. People are making fun of you. You don't think it's true. You've been around here for a hundred years. You've made your mark and now everybody's joking around because you're the idiot who fell asleep on the air.

"I can understand how Mike felt. Radio alone and no one would have known. But he's over it, and should be."

Rosenberg, now a morning host in Florida who knows about a different kind of damage control, saw past it quickly.

"If anybody out there thinks it's easy to do a show every day for five and a half hours without Chris anymore, and command the numbers and revenue that Mike does, then they're nuts," he said. "You know what? He's got kids and he was tired. Big fucking deal. The fact is Mike's an easy target. I was when I was there. A lot of it is his fault because he's an arrogant guy. He's not a bad guy, I know

Mike. I've seen Mike do things for people at The Fan, and to say they were nice is an understatement.

"But I think that some people think he's arrogant, think he's a prick, he's not good with the callers, thinks his shit doesn't stink. Maybe all of that is true. But I really thought that thing was blown way over the top."

That's life in today's day and age. Anyone with an iPhone or iPad can push someone's less-than-stellar moment out to the masses, and peoples' lives can change. In fact, in April of 2013, after video surfaced of Rutgers basketball coach Mike Rice kicking and shoving his players, Francesa often referred to his incident.

"Listen," he said on Wednesday, April 3, the day Rice was fired. "It's amazing how fast these things take off. It happened to me. I know."

In this one September instance for Francesa—given all the benefits with YES—that shift would have been a good day to just be on radio.

"The Internet, 11 years ago when Mike and Chris started on YES, wasn't the force that it is now. Everything's instant. Sometimes it's great, and sometimes it can be a little less than flattering. In this case, it was the latter," said John Filippelli, the president of production and programming at YES.

"I can't take Mike to fault. Mike lives what he does, works a lot of hours. He's got to travel to Manhattan, and he's got kids at home. It's easy to get tired. If it was me, God knows it would have happened more than once.

"So, you know what? If your body gets the better of you in that situation and it's closing your eyes, it happens. If it wasn't for our cameras, it never would have happened. But look, the people that want to take a shot at you will take a shot. The downside of celebrity is that people like to do that. Sometimes the shots are deserved. Sometimes they're ridiculous. That's celebrity. That's society."

Francesa has since opened up about it. In fact, in his interview, he and Julio shared some laughs somewhere on the Long Island

Expressway, when a memorable night at Yankee Stadium, not long after "Sleepgate," came up in conversation.

"Mike, I'd like to talk about the Yankees game that you have mentioned, not long after you closed your eyes on air. The night where the fan was calling over to you all night. It speaks to the situation, and moving beyond it, yet always remembering it."

"Hahahaha, hahahaha, I don't hear it put that way often. That's good," Francesa said. "That's good, but you can say falling asleep, I don't care. Hey a lot of people remember that story acutely. I'm driving with Julio right now and Julio wanted to kill that guy!"

Francesa, at this point, makes Julio a part of the conversation. He looks over at him and says to his driver, *"He's talking about that day at the Stadium where that guy rode me the whole game."*

"I'm telling you, Julio wanted to kill him. I just said 'Let him do it. Let him talk, it's okay.' I knew I was going to have some confrontations that way because that got so much attention. Nothing I ever did—and I've done some things—got *that much* attention, and I get a lot of attention just by nature. I'm just one of those people who gets a lot of attention. That time, I got so much. It was unbelievable.

"Everywhere I went, that's all I heard about. I knew there was going to be some remarks and I'm telling you, I sat there and Julio goes to the games with me. Julio has been with me a long time, works full time, driving me...he's my driver. When we go to games, he's the biggest Yankee fan in the world and he sits with me. In our group, he always has a ticket. That's part of the deal. And frankly he was going to go over to this guy. And I said 'You just got to let him go. As long as he doesn't offend anybody, as long as he doesn't get over the line or really get out of hand' where the security would have stopped him.

"The security asked me during the game if the guy was bothering me. I said 'No, let him sound off. Let him say what he wants. It's fine.' It's funny. I just took it. You have to. That's part of the deal. You ride a player when he's going bad, you know? That guy wanted to ride me. He rode me the whole night. At the end of the night, when I got up and left, so many people were so upset about it. I was like 'Let it go.'

"I didn't like it, but you know what? Sometimes you have to take your medicine. That's the way it goes. Sometimes you have to pay. So, I did."

Then he moved on, even if no one else did. On September 21, as Russo pointed out, Francesa won the 2012 National Association of Broadcasters Marconi Radio's Major Market Personality of the Year Award. On April 2, 2013, he signed a multiyear contract extension that locked him up at WFAN for "several years to come," according to CBS. And ever so slowly, "Sleepgate" finally drifted off.

"The way I look at FAN now, I have one more chapter to write," Francesa said. "There will be chapters written after I'm gone. But there's probably one more—maybe two—to be written during my time."

Indeed, the new deal put the retirement talk on ice, and also squashed the rumors of a reunion with Russo.

"Mike's been such an integral part of the radio station," Spitz said, "and I hope personally he's with the radio station for a long, long time."

He's not alone.

"Mike does a great job and when it's all said and done, you can have Jim Rome, you can have Dan Patrick, you can have any of these guys, whomever you think is a big deal in this business. You can have them," Rosenberg said.

"For me, Sid Rosenberg, Mike Francesa is the best of all time."

13

Graduation Day

When Mike [Francesa] and I started going to the Super Bowl, very few stations would go and broadcast all week like we did. We went to New Orleans after the '89 season, and we worked out of the lobby of the Hyatt by ourselves. Now when you go to the Super Bowl, you see a million radio stations, a million different outlets. That was not the case early on. I do not notice [WFAN's impact] on a day-in, day-out basis, because I'm not paying too much attention to it. But at the Super Bowl, it does dawn on me a little bit. I look around and say, 'Geez, it used to be just us, and now look at the place.' Sports radio has really taken off and I suppose we had a lot to do with that.

—CHRIS RUSSO

CHRIS CARLIN DELIVERED PRESCRIPTIONS for Hasler's Pharmacy in his hometown of Chatham Township, New Jersey, in the early 1990s. The twins down the street needed their penicillin and Mom couldn't leave the house? Not a problem—Carlin was your man. The elderly woman caught a case of poison ivy after working in the yard? No sweat—Carlin was on the case.

On a good day, the jovial Garden State native would have a full list of stops to make, because that meant he could listen to WFAN all day. It was those days that truly helped shape his career path, one that had to include a stop in Astoria, Queens, at some point.

"I loved it. Whether it was Mike and Chris or someone else, I was listening. I couldn't get enough of it. For me, a Jersey guy, what they were talking about was everything I cared about, and I knew then and there that I wanted in," he said with determination some 20 years later. "I didn't know how, I didn't know when. I just knew I wanted in."

That was enough to fuel Carlin, who struggled early in his college days with what he called "academic issues." Eventually he pushed through three years at Hobart College in Geneva, New York, gaining invaluable experience along the way. He learned his way around the studio, he learned how to do play-by-play, and he put himself in the best possible position to succeed.

Carlin was fortunate enough to land a spot calling games for the Geneva Cubs, a Class A minor league baseball team, while he was still in school. As is the case with most clubs in the minors, broadcasters also hold several jobs for a team.

"The first summer, I interned in '93 for $17 a game, and I didn't get paid when I did the radio," he said. "In '94, they moved to Williamsport, Pennsylvania, and they invited me back. I worked in the front office and did games. In '95, same thing. It was fun. But I graduated in '95, so at the end of the summer, it was over. I had no job to speak of, no interview, no nothing."

He wasn't about to go back to Hasler's, though. Not then. Not ever. Carlin at that point was closer to New York City than ever, and he was determined to continue chasing his dream.

"I sent in for an internship at WFAN, and I got the call sometime in July," he said. "We were on a road trip. I think we were in Vermont and I got a phone call from this guy, Eddie Scozzare. Three or four days later, I was in there for an interview. I had to drive to New York for the interview, and that was new to me. Outside of going to Shea Stadium, I had never been to Queens in my life, even though I grew up in Jersey."

Of course, many opportunities are accompanied by obstacles, and Carlin faced a big one.

"Before I came in for the interview, he told me I had to get college credit for the internship," Carlin said. "So that was a problem, since I was already out of school. So, I sent resumes to mid-level colleges looking for a broadcaster. I called, no joke, about 50 colleges in New York, New Jersey, and Pennsylvania, just looking for a school where I could take a course. Finally, Bloomsburg University in Pennsylvania was where I was able to get it. I paid them $500 and got the credit for the internship."

The rest is history. Carlin got his foot in the door and no one was likely to be strong enough to push the larger-than-life character out of it anytime soon. The man Russo and Francesa would later tab "The Continent," Carlin took on role after role at The Fan, establishing an identity, cultivating his craft, and loving every minute of it.

"I got very, very lucky with who I was working for and how it all worked out," Carlin said humbly. "Hard work created some of it, yes, but truly there was luck in there. A lot of it."

Sid Rosenberg agreed.

"I happen to love Chris. He's doing a great job. He's always done a great job. But Chris Carlin's whole career is because of me," Rosenberg said with a laugh. "I got fired from *Imus in the Morning*, [then] he did the updates. I got fired from the Giants, [then] he did the Giants. Every time I got fired, they gave Chris Carlin my gigs!

Whatever he does for the rest of his life, he should send me a check every freakin' month!"

But like many other employees at WFAN, Carlin eventually found greener pastures elsewhere. It took a heck of an opportunity, of course, to leave the station, but Carlin eventually was compelled to move on to bigger and better things. He is now the pre- and post-game television host for the New York Mets on SportsNet New York. All of those on-air shifts at WFAN, when he learned to joke when a laugh was needed and to be stern when it was time to be serious, paid off for The Continent, whose physical appearance doesn't fit the traditional TV star mold.

"When I first came over and started doing it, it was a process," Carlin said. "It's one thing to do *Loudmouths* and be a guest on *Daily News Live*, because they want me to go out there and have fun. But then you do the Mets pre- and postgame and it's a completely different role than I've ever done before. But, hey, they didn't hire me because I was 'Johnny Anchor,' clearly. They kind of thought I had an 'everyguy' quality to me. Fat and bald probably lends itself to that. I get a lot more out of it than I ever thought I would. Again, I never gave a thought of going to television. I've just been very fortunate in that regard."

Carlin still has a presence at WFAN. He does spot shows, especially around the holidays, and his smiling face also received airtime on the station's 25th anniversary show in 2012, hosted by Francesa. Carlin is still the same guy. He makes others laugh—most of the time, by making fun of himself—and he still has a boatload of sports knowledge that plays well on radio as well as television.

"It's still a fun thing for me to do on occasion. There's no doubt I miss doing a radio show every day from that standpoint, because it's a lot of fun, the interaction you get," he said. "It's unlike anything else. SNY has been rewarding in different ways, too, but in a lot of ways, The Fan is always going to be home. I spent 13 years there."

Others didn't wait that long to pack up their WFAN experience and carve out a niche somewhere else. It's all about timing in this business, and when the opportunity knocks, you have to listen.

Kevin Burkhardt certainly did. Another New Jersey native raised on The Fan, Burkhardt was also a jack-of-all-trades at the station as a youngster, taking on whatever roles needed to be filled. Sports updates, the occasional overnight show, you name it, Burkhardt wanted a piece of it.

And how can you blame him? After graduating from William Paterson University in his home state and feeling he'd built a foundation for a television or a radio career, he found himself selling cars at Pine Belt Chevrolet in Eatontown, New Jersey. Yep, good, old Eatontown, right smack-dab in the middle of Monmouth County—59 miles away from Astoria but a whole world away.

"WFAN was the mountaintop. When I started out, I was working at a thousand-watt radio station that was a daytimer. We talked high school sports and did high school games. So, yeah, WFAN was the Mecca. That's where you wanted to get to. But I was nowhere near it," Burkhardt said. "I was basically part-time at WCBS radio at that point, and I had gotten fed up with the business, so I started selling cars."

If you needed a brand-new SUV to handle the roads of the Jersey Shore, Burkhardt was your guy. He always had a smile and a handshake and was always happy to let you take a test drive. But personally he longed to drive somewhere else.

"Sometimes, things change with a call," he said. "I gave a call to [former WFAN program director] Eric Spitz. He's a great friend, but he's also been a great mentor for me. I called him up and said,

'I think I'm good enough to work on The Fan, and I want to get a tryout.' And he said, 'Okay.'"

Burkhardt was stunned. Confused, even. Was that an "Okay, thanks for calling, get lost, kid?" Or did Spitz really want him to come in and take a shot?

"So, sure enough, I went in and sat down with John Minko. It's so wild how I'm around pro athletes every day and I'm not starstruck, but I was starstruck sitting down with John Minko, talking with him, and seeing everyone around The Fan. It was just a really cool thing. Having a chance to meet all those people that you listened to forever, in this place that you wanted to get to for your entire career, was wild. It was just cool to be in that building."

And though he left the building that day, it wasn't for long. Burkhardt, equipped with a deep, demonstrative radio voice, hit the air running at WFAN. He made friends with Russo, he developed strong ties to his callers, and for a while there, the thought was that he was working his way toward a permanent spot on a daily show.

"Spitzy hired me on a part-time basis and I was going to do updates, a little reporting, and some talk shows here and there. I remember the first day that I went on. I did updates on a Saturday morning. You're there from 6:00 in the morning, and I'm not a morning person, but I was all kinds of excited," he said. "Russo was hosting that morning at 10:00—that's when he did Saturday shows. It was just so cool to hear him say for the first time, 'We got the update now. There's somebody new. Kevin Burkhardt is here.' I felt like I had arrived. Chris was great from Day 1."

But there were still bills to pay. Burkhardt may have arrived, but it was only a part-time arrival, and there were still people down in Jersey who needed their Chevy Cruzes.

"I made my debut with Chris on a Saturday, the next week I was doing updates for Mike and Chris, and then the next day? Back to the car dealership," he said.

But Burkhardt's star was rising, and although that permanent gig never materialized—Evan Roberts eventually landed the spot next to Joe Benigno in the midday—it was just a matter of time before someone else saw the upside in Burkhardt.

Turns out, that outlet was SNY. Today, when you turn on one of myriad Mets broadcasts on that station, you see Carlin on the pre- and postgame shows and Burkhardt as the field reporter. They've moved from The Fan to the field.

"I was certainly a little nervous about leaving," said Burkhardt, who also moved on to do NFL play by play on Fox in 2013. "I went to school more for television than I did for radio. I always liked TV more but radio just became my natural path in school. It became my first love. For me, the timing worked out great. I could see that Evan was going to get a chance at the next big opportunity, which obviously came up. Those opportunities don't come often. I enjoyed the hell out my time there and I learned so much and did so many great things, but in the terms of career advancement, it was just perfect timing for me. If I stayed there, who knows what happens? But I think the beauty of it is everyone there was so supportive when I left and is still supportive. I'm good friends with all those guys.

"I think it was time to move on for me but it was a happy feeling. This industry can be cutthroat, but I never felt for one second that anybody there didn't have my back. Everyone did everything they could for the show to go on and make it entertaining. Even now, all the people that are there who I've never met or maybe meet for the first time because they know I worked there, it's kind of like a brotherhood. We have this bond. Whether it was working together at 3:00 in the morning on a Saturday night or whenever, there is something about that place that I will always take with me. The place always felt like home."

Seeing former WFAN staff members succeed elsewhere is a point of pride for Mark Chernoff.

"A lot of people have done really well, and I think it makes us all feel very good that The Fan call letters mean something elsewhere," Chernoff said. "In a lot of those cases, yes, we nurtured those people, and some have stayed, and some have moved on and gotten national recognition and national jobs. We're certainly very proud of that."

Steve Levy was another WFAN staffer who eventually spread his wings on another station. Long before he became the anchor on ESPN's *SportsCenter* or called some of the most dramatic Stanley Cup playoff games for the network, Levy was something of a precursor to Burkhardt and Carlin.

A New York native who graduated from SUNY Oswego in 1987, Levy, who was also a local sports anchor on New York's CBS Channel 2, eventually snagged a pinch-hitting role at WFAN and soon became part of a groundbreaking show at a groundbreaking station.

It's a given today, but a show on which fans can get updates from every NFL stadium all Sunday long was new in the early 1990s. Scores weren't so easy to come by then, and most statistics weren't available until Monday morning's newspaper. But a show on which you could get all of that in real time, with reporters on-site at the stadiums? Genius.

"I wound up being the first guy in the country to do that type of NFL show," Levy said of what WFAN now calls *The NFL in Action*. "Eddie Coleman did it after me. Every station in the country does it now. But I'm pretty sure we were the first to ever do it that way, with a stringer at every game. It was a really cool concept and I think my role, quite frankly, was to stay out of the way. When we got ESPN Radio, Mike Tirico and I did a similar show. But like many things, I suppose, it started on The Fan."

And it still continues today.

"I work mainly with the Mets and most people associate me with that. But I still get a lot of people who listen every Sunday to the NFL show," Coleman said. "Even in this day and age, when everything is on your phone and you can get updates left and right, people say, 'I love being in my car listening to what's going on at the games.' It's fun to do. But it's crazy. The one thing about doing the show is that it keeps you busy the entire time. But it's gratifying to know everyone has something like that and we were one of the first to do it."

Levy certainly used his time at The Fan as a springboard. It wasn't long into his run there before ESPN came calling. In fact, he had discussions with the empire on more than one occasion. But he wasn't so sure that moving to ESPN's campus in Bristol, Connecticut, was what he wanted to do. He was, after all, a New Yorker, and was living his dream in his city. He was single, he was enjoying the life, and well...

"I did not want to go," Levy said. "I grew up in the city. I was on The Fan four nights a week. I was doing Friday and Saturday on Channel 2 for CBS. I had a life. I was living in a high-rise in Manhattan and I thought it was great. I did not want to come to ESPN. My agent at the time said, 'Hey, listen, I got an offer from ESPN.' Well, we actually turned it down."

How's that for the power of WFAN?

"Yeah, I loved the station, loved New York. I think six months later, ESPN came back with a better offer and I still didn't want to go. So we went to Channel 2 and said, 'I don't want to go. Don't make me go. But I want to be on TV more.' They were like, 'Steve, you're 24, 25. You can't be the number-one guy on CBS in New York. It just doesn't work that way.'

"In the end, my agent said, 'This is ESPN. They're not going to come back a third time.' And so I left. But I was crushed. I did not

want to leave. Most of the people come to Connecticut from different parts of the country and that is their lifelong dream, to be on or
at ESPN. Growing up in New York, I did not feel that way. I was all
about the city, about WFAN, about the Garden, and all that stuff. It
was with much apprehension that I moved to Bristol."

You can say that it worked out for Levy, of course, and he'll be
the first to admit that now. ESPN has made him a megastar. But it
definitely took some time to adjust to Bristol. That toddlin' town,
it ain't.

"I remember, way back when, I went to a movie by myself on a
Tuesday in Bristol, and I was literally the only person in the theater,"
Levy said with a laugh. "And the guy running the projector banged
on the glass and said, 'Hey, are you ready?' I said 'Yeah, roll it.' They
actually showed the movie just for me. That's a true story.

"By the way, it was the best move I ever made careerwise, life-
wise. I've had 19 years here and I would sign up for 19 more if they
offered it to me. When I went in, there was only ESPN. There was
no ESPN2 even. So, we've come a long way."

So has Don La Greca.

A native of Hawthorne, New Jersey, La Greca was a die-hard
sports fan with a proud, pulverizing broadcasting voice in the works
when The Fan started to make waves in the 1980s. He was at Ramapo
College in the Garden State, and he was never far from a radio.

"I was obsessed. A sports-radio station? I went nuts because
that's what I lived for," he said. "So, I kind of mimicked a lot of what
they were doing early on at my college station. I wanted to pick up
tips and figure out how I could do this for a living. I listened to Art
Rust Jr. and his *Sportstalk* show, but that was just a few hours every
day. To know that I could listen constantly to WFAN, it was a whole
new world. I would always take classes in the afternoon so I could
listen to Steve Somers until 5:00 in the morning. Just like a kid who

picked up a baseball bat and wanted to play major league baseball, I looked at that as my majors. I did everything I could to get to what I thought was the paradise of the business in sports radio."

It wasn't an easy path for La Greca but it was a rewarding one all the same. He hooked up with an outfit called Sports Phone and eventually landed a gig doing updates on 1010 WINS, an AM news station. An ultimate destination WINS was not, of course. But it was a broader platform and a place where more people—important people—could hear him.

"I did that for six months and Mark Chernoff heard one of my updates," La Greca said. "It was right at the time when The Fan needed an overnight sports anchor. I got a phone call from Steve Malzberg [of Shadow Traffic and Sports] in the morning and he said, 'Get your ass into the studio right now and make a tape for Mark Chernoff. He's going to make a decision right away.' So I ran over to Shadow Sports, which is on Route 17 in East Rutherford, right across from the Meadowlands. Steve gave me a studio and I jumped in there and recorded updates until I had a perfect one. I gave it to Steve and a couple days later he said, 'Yup, Mark loves it. Get over there and start training.'"

It was another dream realized.

"I couldn't believe it. I went over for training with the update anchors there—John Minko and Bob Wischusen. I met Chris Russo, it was just...I can't describe it," La Greca said with a reflective pause. "It literally was like that 19-, 20-year-old kid getting called up to the majors and meeting all the guys he worshipped. I went from doing updates part-time at WINS to being the overnight update anchor at WFAN in a 10-day span. It was really crazy."

La Greca was a fit on The Fan because of where he grew up, because of his love for New York sports, and because of his encyclopedic memory. But it took a dangerous situation to give him his first shot at hosting his own show.

"My big break came when Joe Benigno's house caught fire," he said. "I guess it was 2001, toward the end of the time I was there. Joe's house burned down and he couldn't work. I was working the day shift and it was the day that Dale Earnhardt Sr. died. So I went home, showered, took a nap, came back, and did the overnight. It was all Dale Earnhardt, and luckily I was a bit of a NASCAR fan, so I handled that. Joe ended up being out the whole week, so I got to do that week and it really gave me the confidence that I could do this."

Down the dial on 1050 AM, ESPN had launched a New York–centric sports station that would include nationally simulcast programs, but also local sports talk, as well as NBA, NHL, and NFL games. The project was a perfect fit for La Greca. Today, his voice is a fixture on ESPN, which is now all-Spanish on 1050 and English on 98.7 FM. He is the cohost of *The Michael Kay Show*, which competes with Mike Francesa's *Mike's On*. And La Greca is the rinkside reporter on the New York Rangers radio network, as well. He is also the team's backup play-by-play man to Kenny Albert.

The voices of Albert and La Greca traditionally weave through a Rangers game with efficiency and effortlessness. But while most people associate Albert with either his family of broadcasters—including his legendary father, Marv—or his work as an NFL play-by-play man for Fox, it is sometimes forgotten that he, too, spent time at WFAN. And like the others, long before he made it to station, he was in awe of it.

"I remember July of '87 so well," Albert said. "WFAN came on the air and I was working for a basketball team, the Staten Island Stallions of the United States Basketball League, at the time. I was doing public relations and stats work for them, working in the office. I was so excited about this all-sports station coming on the air that on the actual day it went on, I bought one of those big boom-box radios to the office. There I was, walking into the office in Staten

Island, carrying one of those boom boxes with a cassette recorder. I actually have the tape somewhere; that's how into it I was. I taped Suzyn Waldman's first update and whatever else happened in that first hour."

Albert started at WFAN as an associate producer for *Mets Extra*, which was a great opportunity to network. Years later, when he became the full-time voice of the Rangers and the club's broadcasting rights still belonged to WFAN, Albert's play-by-play calls were aired on Sports Radio 66.

"You look at the people who have come through there, and the people who are there now—what they started at The Fan is truly incredible," Albert said. "I don't think I ever would have imagined sports radio would be as big as it's gotten. When people ask me what it was like growing up in a sports-media family, I always tell them that I felt like our dinner table was like the first all-sports radio station.

"When I think back to my teenage years, I would get all my sports news, pretty much, from newspapers and magazines. It was from the local news. Those sportscasters at 6:00 and 11:00 were the face of sports in your town. But if you ask a kid these days, the face of sports in New York would be a Mike Francesa or one of the guys at The Fan.

"The station is *that* strong and the talent there is *that* good."

14

Let's Go to Rego Park and Talk to Doris

I've always treasured the calls, and I think it comes from my father. My father was a pretty gregarious guy. Being friendly, being approachable, I think it's part of my personality. I think callers appreciate that, and we feel the same way. Give them a chance to talk, give them a chance to communicate, try not to put yourself in a situation where you're above the call. We're all talking sports—this is not nuclear physics. We're not trying to split the atom. I realized long ago that they were a big part of the show; they're part of my weaponry. None of us are going to get very far without the callers. —CHRIS RUSSO

JIM LAMPLEY RECEIVED THE FIRST TASTE OF IT, some 26 years ago. It was Lampley who officially opened the phone lines at WFAN to the outside world after Suzyn Waldman inaugurated the station with a sports update. He didn't know what was on the other side of those lines. No one did. Some were sure to be loud, obnoxious, and perhaps a bit off their rockers. Others were sure to be knowledgeable, articulate, and thoughtful. Somewhere in the middle would probably be the norm.

For a format as innovative as WFAN and all-sports radio was back in 1987, the unknown that was the calling public was an absolute perfect fit.

"We had a little bit of everything with those early callers, but they are all really fond memories because of the fun and the pure whimsy of a lot of it, and how we were able to build shows around them," said Lampley, now the face of boxing broadcasting and HBO Sports. "I was making things up as I went along, and we got away with it. It was tremendous fun. I learned what talk radio is. You use the callers as material to build on because they're the lunatic fringe. You know, of all the people who listen in to talk radio—in sports or politics—fewer than 1 percent would actually pick up the phone and call in. So even though you're taking calls day after day and it feels like everybody out there is calling in, that isn't the case. They're the lunatic fringe. So you treat them as program material, and they usually can't get enough of it. They keep coming back for more."

Indeed, they are a loyal bunch, and over the years, many of their names became identifiable to the rest of the audience, no matter which WFAN show they called into. "Short Al from Brooklyn." "Eli from Westchester." "Jerome from Manhattan." "Mike from Montclair." "Bruce from Bayside." "Miriam from Forest Hills."

Each had their own schtick. Each had their own favorite teams. Some calls—and callers—were better than others, but as the years went by and the hosts began to pass through the revolving door at WFAN, it became the callers, the people who completed the other end of what longtime afternoon host Chris Russo calls the "two-way sports talk telephone number," who displayed true loyalty to The Fan.

"I will never forget them, and in some cases, vice versa," Lampley said with a laugh. "Every once in a while, a person comes up to me and says, 'I'm Bruce from Flushing.' I get that every once in a while, and I can't help but smile and chat about the old times. I'll be in a group somewhere and somebody will say, 'Did you know Jim was the first voice on WFAN?' and people go, 'Huh?' They have trouble associating me with that. But not those callers, those listeners who were and are vital to WFAN. People get hooked on it. People love it. And I don't think that it will ever go away."

Joe Benigno concurs. And how can he not? He was one of those callers for so many years, one of those mainstays of the so-called lunatic fringe. Week in and week out, "Joe from Saddle River" would jump on the line and scream about the ineptness of the New York Jets; cringe over the free-throw shooting of the New York Knicks; and wonder aloud just who was going to hit leadoff for the New York Mets.

He was so good at it, he made it a career. And nearly 20 years later, here he is, still taking your calls, still thanking you for your calls, and still making the most of the glorious chance he received.

"I get noticed sometimes, but up against Joe? Forget it," said Evan Roberts, Benigno's midday cohost. "Don't let him tell you otherwise—Joe is Elvis. I've hung out with Joe Benigno. He's freakin' Elvis when he walks around town."

It wasn't always that way, though. When Benigno first started out at WFAN—long before he hosted the midday show that bridges *Boomer & Carton* and *Mike's On*, long before he penned his own book about New York sports, and certainly long before he became a fixture on television opinion shows—Benigno was your friendly overnight host. And while he meant a lot to the lunatic fringe, he hadn't yet hit the mainstream.

But that didn't matter to him. To him, it was about the Mets, the Jets, the Knicks, the Rangers...and the callers. He needed them and they needed him. Indeed, he took the torch from his overnight predecessor, Steve Somers, and always held the callers in high regard. It went beyond sports with both Somers and Benigno. Real life often came up with these callers, and if you were a loyal listener of either show, you began to familiarize yourself with those contributors as much as the hosts. In many ways, there wouldn't have been a show without them.

For Benigno and many others, when you talk about those times and those shows and those callers, it begins with a little old lady from Queens who was as unforgettable as she was unmistakable.

"Doris from Rego Park" had an encyclopedic memory of the Mets, and was often given the time to share some of that knowledge. The current state of the lineup, what could be done about the lack of middle relief, the next great prospect to come up from Triple A—you name it, Doris had an opinion about it. She knew her stuff, and with a scratchy, monotone voice and a famous cough that often separated her thoughts, she quickly etched herself into the foundation of this proud station.

"She was one of the key characters on the show. Her love for the Mets and her knowledge of baseball was just tremendous," Benigno said fondly. "Obviously the cough—the constant, constant cough she had because of the illnesses she had—was kind of a trademark of hers, as well. I think that also made her what she was."

Doris Bauer suffered from a condition known as neurofibromatosis, which is a genetically traced disorder that affects nerve tissue. The disease presents a variety of symptoms, and for Doris, one of them was a persistent rasp that helped to define her on the station's air.

"She wasn't the easiest person to get along with all the time. She had a very hard edge to her. I think a lot of it had to do with the bad hand that life dealt her," Benigno said. "But she made herself a celebrity because of the overnight years. I think she was the most celebrated of the callers—certainly to my show. I don't think there's any doubt about it."

In 2003, Bauer passed away at the age of 58, and Benigno broke the news to his listeners on the air. He took some calls about her as the overnight family reminisced. WFAN paid its respects, as well, posting a note on the station's official website that read, "Over the years, Doris has become part of the tapestry of WFAN and a friend to many of the on-air hosts and staff. Her loyalty to this station and her beloved Mets was unmatched."

Doris became such a fixture over the years that it's hard to find someone who doesn't have a story about her.

"Well, she was very knowledgeable. She knew what she was talking about, and she was feisty," said WFAN operations manager Mark Chernoff. "She was a great caller, and we've been lucky with people like her. We've had some very good, very loyal callers but Doris was certainly one of those special people.

"She was such a big Mets fan, and we miss some of the callers that we've lost through the years. Without the callers, the radio station doesn't survive. They are our lifeblood. I've always said that from Day 1. They are the people who really make up the pulse of the radio station. Our hosts know what the hot topic is. They relate to it, they get into it, they get guests on it, and they do monologues on it. But it's how the callers relate to that topic that actually sets the tone and really gives it even more direction."

Ian Eagle, who took on many different roles at WFAN before moving onto CBS Sports, among other places, received many calls from Doris and has forgotten very few of them.

"My favorite caller, back in the day, was 'Vinny from Queens,' who apparently died after being hit by a car. Just a tragic story,"

Eagle recalled. "He was informed, level-headed, full of information, opinionated. It was Yankees and Yankees only. He specialized in one topic and he knocked it out of the park every time he called. 'Doris from Rego Park,' same deal as Vinny. She specialized in one topic, and she was great at it. It was Mets only. And she also specialized in a terrible whooping cough. 'Ian, cough, cough, I tell ya somethin', the Mets need a...'"

Are some hosts short with callers at times? Absolutely. But most of the time—especially with the regular callers—there's a respect and an admiration on both sides.

"'Roger from New Haven,' 'Bruce from Bayside,' 'Rob from Lake Success,' 'Bruce from Flushing,' 'Leslie from Fort Lee,' 'Ralph from Manhattan,' 'James from Manhattan'—who hates the Yankees and loves his Baltimore Orioles. You go up and down the line, there are so many callers for me who are regular and really add to what I'm doing," said Marc Malusis, a former producer for *Mike and the Mad Dog* who now hosts an overnight show on WFAN and also contributes to the CBS Sports Radio Network. "The callers are such an asset to the station, and I never forget that. When you don't hear from somebody in a while, it's good to hear their voice because you want to make sure they're doing all right. It's part of the charm of sports radio, that people get to talk a little smack and get to rub people the wrong way and have a good time with it. Sports are meant to be entertaining, and that's what we do. Certainly the callers are a necessary and tremendous part of it."

That's certainly not lost on Russo. He can incense some callers when he's in an ornery mood, but at his core, he cares for them, he appreciates them, and he knows what they've done for his career through the years.

"Remember, I was in Jacksonville, Florida. We didn't have a ton of callers on a day-in, day-out basis. We only had two phone lines,"

Russo said with a chuckle. "Jacksonville, Florida, is what it is; it's a small town. Calls, to me, were precious."

He's not alone. A host such as Ed Coleman, an original WFAN-er who is now the beat reporter for the Mets, doesn't get too many opportunities to take calls. For Coleman and others like him, those shows represent catch-up time with some of his long-lost friends. It goes beyond just a host-caller relationship. Bonds grow over time, and when you have passionate, proud people on both ends, they become stronger.

"I'll give you two favorites," Coleman said not long after the shootings in Newtown, Connecticut, at Sandy Hook Elementary School. "One of them I've been thinking about over the last couple of days, and that's 'John from Sandy Hook.' I don't know if he lived in Newtown, but the Sandy Hook that was part of his moniker, that came from Connecticut. He was a great caller. He was an older caller, I think he was in his seventies, and you knew it meant a lot for him to call in. He was up on sports, but he was also a historian. Anytime he called, I loved it.

"The other guy, and he's probably been mentioned by several people, is 'Vinny from Queens.' He was a classic. He called all the time, and then it stopped, and several people at the station were concerned. Lot of guys took that to the air, and asked where he was. Vinny from Queens' sister actually called one day to tell us he had been hit by a car and died. We were stunned. He was such a big Yankees fan. A tremendous caller. He just knew everything cold. He got angry at stuff but he'd have a rational mind. I always loved talking to Vinny."

Chris Carlin has made a career of trading on his "everyguy" quality, as he puts it. Leave it to the guy who has "I don't roll outta bed this handsome" on his Twitter page to truly appreciate what the callers bring to the table. Recall that before graduating to *Imus in the Morning* and eventually landing a television gig on SportsNet New York, Carlin was the overnight host at WFAN.

"Yeah, Joe Benigno moved to middays and I got the overnight. I had it for only a few months but I loved it, man. You understood what Joe and Steve talked about when they talked about the callers, when they talked about the overnight as a family," Carlin said. "And those guys were the die-hards, the people with insomnia. 'Eddie from Staten Island' is one of my all-time favorite callers. We would go at it about the Knicks. I loved 'Eric from the Bronx.' I love those guys. It was me learning from them, really. The overnight was where I learned to have fun.

"The first couple of times I was on the air, Chernoff hated my show. He hated it, trust me. Why did he hate it? It was way too stiff. I was way too worried about using every little fact and figure that I could. And at some point later that year, when it was clear he didn't like me on the air, I just let it fly. I was on weekend overnights, and I took a bunch of calls and just had fun with them. And that's when he started to like me."

"Frank from Massapequa" comes up in a lot of conversations. He's tough on his hosts, and leave it to a character like Evan Roberts to illustrate that. A regular caller like Frank can test his show prep.

"Something will happen in a game, and I'll say, 'Yeah, so-and-so is going to call about that,'" Roberts said. "After Jets games, you know you're going to hear from 'Ira in Staten Island.' One of my favorite callers is a guy named 'Frank in Massapequa,' who will call up and complain about something every day. It's usually something Joe said or I said, and it's usually anti-Mets or anti-Knicks or anti-Jets. But it's always a complaint…and I love it! Even though it is always negative, it freakin' entertains me like nothing else. When a caller calls up and says 'You're an idiot, and here's why,' that's my favorite. Whenever I see Frank on the screen, I try to figure out what Joe or I said or did that he's going to complain about.

"The calls are tremendous, especially after emotional wins or losses, because you relate to them. One of the most important bedrocks of the station is the callers, the regulars and the first-timers. I do get a kick when somebody says he's a first-time caller because he's been listening to the station forever, probably, and for some reason, something happened on this show that caused this person to call in for the first time."

One thing you don't hear much of—and this is a credit to the board operators and the producers—is callers getting out of line. Yelling? Sure. But it's usually in good taste, and the callers are usually sober. That's not always a given on the overnight shift, when the bars are closing and the host is looking to take a call or two.

"That was a concern of mine," said Jody McDonald, an original host on WFAN who started out doing weekend overnights. "You are in the hands of your producer, who is on the firing line, picking up the phone with these guys. Now, if you haven't taken a call in half an hour, and somebody calls in and he's borderline, what do you do?

"Luckily, WFAN hit the ground running. The ratings weren't always there, but the interaction always seemed to be there. I really never lacked for telephone calls. So my producer could be good and diligent and try and screen out those kinds of guys. Every once in a while, we'd take a chance and roll with a guy we had suspicions had had a cocktail or two, and we'd try and make it entertaining and humorous and have some fun with the guy. But it was much less of a problem than I originally thought it could have been when I took the job."

It does take all kinds to build a caller base, so consider WFAN's regulars one big melting pot. Eagle recalls one personal connection he made that he'll never forget.

"I think it was during one of my first weeks doing the overnight. I came out of the building after a show, and there's a guy standing there with a brown paper bag," Eagle said. "I think it was 'Tony from Rockaway Beach.' He said, 'Hey, are you Ian Eagle?' At that point, I had done no television work, my picture had never been in the paper, no one would ever know what I look like. It's 6:00 on a Sunday morning. He said, 'I hear you like calzones. I hear you like broccoli rolls.' I said, 'Yeah, who doesn't like broccoli rolls?'

"He said, 'I was listening and you mentioned it, so I got some for ya. I got some sauce for ya, too. But that's in my own personal Tupperware, so I'm going to need that back.' I said, 'Oh, I'll get that back to ya. No problem.'

"It was the middle of winter. I wasn't married yet, but my fiancée at the time was living in the city on 80th and First. I was still getting used to working that shift and I would go back there after these shows and get right to bed. So I put this bag outside on the terrace—the smell was something else—and we go on about our day. We get back and she must've gone outside and found it. She said, 'What the hell is this? There's a brown bag outside here…and it stinks!'

"So, the shit had frozen. All I'm thinking is that I've got to return this guy's Tupperware and the shit's frozen inside it. So, I try to collect my thoughts and I tell my fiancée the background. She said, 'You're not going to eat it are you?' I said, 'No, I'm not going to eat it. I don't know what the hell this could be. This guy might hate me for all I know.'

"So I was working Monday through Friday back at The Fan, and the guy calls the newsroom! 'Hey Ian, how'd you like the dinner?'

'Great calzones. Maybe the best I ever had.'

'Yeah…you got that Tupperware? I need it back, like I said.'

"At this point, I was thinking to myself, *Okay, I have to get back, make sure I can find this Tupperware, defrost it, and then bring it back to the station. This is unbelievable!* Somehow, I did it, but that was the kind of one-on-one connections you would make with the listeners and callers back then. It's crazy when you think about it.

"But it is a great place for the callers and the hosts. There's no other place like it. Obviously, now it's been copied. There are more sports radio stations than you know what to do with. The Fan really was the original, though, and it was in the right town with the right audience. For the most part, after they went through that first initial shuffle, they had the right kind of hosts. It was the perfect combination.

"And it's those types—the Tonys [from Rockaway Beach] of the world—who were there every step of the way."

And isn't that the primary reason behind the station, the core vision of a dream some 26 years old?

"The fans are the ones going to the games. They're the ones listening to the games on the radio, watching them on TV, and they're the ones that we need to help us sustain who we are. That's why we're The Fan—it's for them, and it's just a great name," Chernoff said. "I'm sure they thought of that when the name was created. But that name is really for the fans, for the people who listen and call in, and not everybody is a caller. But everybody is a potential caller, and we treat them as such.

"Because without them, we do not survive."

Afterword

The future? Long-term, there are changes coming. There are some tough decisions that Mark Chernoff is going to have to make. I don't know how much longer Mike Francesa really wants to do this. I don't know how much longer Boomer Esiason wants to do this. Right on down the line. Joe Benigno is pushing 60 years old, which is hard to believe. Steve Somers is older. So, obviously, it has to get younger. I think you start with Evan Roberts as a young anchor to the station, and maybe work your way out from there. All I know is that what we have now is—and has been—pretty darn successful. And we just have to keep pumping it out until something gives way.

—JERRY RECCO

JERRY RECCO CAN EASILY DISSECT DIFFERENT ERAS OF WFAN, having lived through many of them. A sports nut who grew up in Hazlet, New Jersey, longing to be a morning news anchor at the only station that *truly* mattered to him, Recco joined The Fan as an intern in 1997 and now lives his dream as the quick-witted, unflappable update man on *Boomer & Carton.*

Sixteen years has taught him a lot, and it starts with knowing his role—and loving it.

"I've accomplished what I *always* wanted. I have zero interest in being a talk show host. I have no interest in being a reporter. I've been there, done that," Recco said. "This is *it*. This *is* what I want to do."

It's hard to blame him. After all, he's quite good at it, having learned to roll with the punches that go with a program Boomer Esiason affectionately calls "a fraternity house," and he still gets home early enough to spend time with his family. Not a bad life. So, as the years unfold at the station's posh studio on 345 Hudson Street in Manhattan, it's likely you'll see Recco—or Rello, as Craig Carton calls him—in a similar seat.

For others? Different story.

Indeed, a younger generation will eventually man the microphones at WFAN. Maybe Carton and Evan Roberts will be joined by homegrown talents such as Marc Malusis and Sweeny Murti in a permanent weekday lineup. Maybe hungry upstarts who won The Fan's "Fantasy Phenom" contest, such as John Jastremski and Joe Giglio, graduate to the next level. Maybe former producer Sal Licata returns as a big-time host. In any case, there appear to be enough at-bats for up-and-coming talent, between overnight shifts, spot weekend duty, and potential work on WFAN's partner station, the CBS Sports Radio Network.

But as the station looks to the future, there are other questions this innovative outfit faces as sports radio continues to flourish:

Will The Fan watch its relationship with the New York Mets come to an end? And would that mean the New York Yankees take over that coveted position? Contracts for both teams ran out in 2013.

Will management decide to move the entire WFAN operation over to the FM dial—on 101.9—leaving 660 to the CBS outfit? And would *"Sports Radio 101.9"* work as a jingle as well as *"Sports Radio 66"* did for parts of four decades? There were reports and social media buzz that hinted as much in 2013.

And with his SiriusXM contract set to expire prior to the 2013 football season, would Chris Russo consider a return to terrestrial radio? With The Fan's daytime lineup set, a reunion with Mike Francesa seemed out of the question. But the notion the Mad Dog could end up at the competition—ESPN New York—gained some summer traction.

To be sure, the opposition at 98.7 FM isn't going anywhere. The station that has broadcast rights to three important New York teams—the Jets, Knicks, and Rangers—could add a baseball contract, and has struck a robust balance between syndicated and local programming.

"We're on the map and we're making inroads," ESPN midday host Don La Greca said. "I've gotten the sense over the last couple of years that we were something easy to make fun of, and not be threatened by, to where they legitimately believe we're coming now. And they better be careful, because if they slip up, we'll be there to jump in."

All that behind-the-scenes jockeying means better sports radio for New York's listeners, and isn't *that* what everyone's after anyway?

"Everything changes, right? You start to sound old fashioned if you don't want to let some stuff go and move forward in this business," Murti said. "But we have a lot of younger guys now that grew up listening to our radio station. That's a pretty fulfilling thing to be on our air and it will inspire them. For them, it's like growing up *watching* the Yankees, and now, you're *playing* for the Yankees. I like to think of The Fan as a sports team. We're a 25-man roster and everyone does their part.

"We're on all the time. We're everywhere. And we're always going to matter."

Acknowledgments

When I read your first book, I felt like you were right there in front of me. I had heard all the words before, but now they were in print for everyone to see. It reminded me of when we were in college and you could write any story of any kind, and you always pushed everyone else to be better writers along the way. Some things never change.

—MIKE WATTICK

THE PUBLISHING INDUSTRY THESE DAYS is in much the same state as the world of journalism. In this new media age, where our phones, tablets, and laptops have replaced newspapers, magazines, and publications worldwide, we find that what was once stable has changed. Jobs aren't as secure. More tasks can be completed every day without that human touch. And overall, with good reason, there is a sense of uneasiness in our daily lives.

One of the natural consequences is that there are fewer books being published, fewer people reading those books, and, in turn, fewer authors being granted the privilege of writing them.

Which is why words cannot fully describe the honor I feel in being able to write my second book in two years. I am incredibly humbled and flattered that after *Battle on the Hudson: The Devils, the Rangers, and the NHL's Greatest Series Ever*, I was able to write this book. These projects have given me the opportunity to share two of my passions and fulfilled two of my professional dreams, all in 13 months.

I will never forget the words of inspiration I received from Mike Vaccaro, a great friend and a greater author, as well as a columnist for the *New York Post*, who told me on the eve of my journey into authordom that "in this case, you get to write the book that you always wanted to write as your first one. That's *something*."

He was right. And to be able to follow that first one up with the *other* book I always wanted to write, well, I cannot tell you how fortunate I am.

But no author completes a task this big without the help of so many different people from so many different walks of life. I would like to acknowledge and thank them.

I'll never forget the first conversation I had with Mark Chernoff, the incredibly talented operations manager at WFAN, who has worked with some of radio's biggest stars throughout a sparkling career and has never lost touch with the public along the way.

"Mark, I've been doing some research and have had several conversations with my publishing company about this," I said. "I would like to write a book about WFAN, span its history, explain its colorful characters, and fully illustrate the world's first true all-sports radio station. But I can't do it without your blessing and your help. It won't be a book without you guys. Does that sound like something the station would be interested in?"

"I have no problem with that at all. Go for it," Chernoff said. "But I have to tell you, this isn't the first time someone has come to me with this idea. Several people have asked this question, I have given them our blessing, and then I never hear from them again."

So, with that as my inspiration, I went to work and began the business of interviewing some of the most entertaining figures in sports media. What a joy it was to hear the razor-sharp memories of many of the original WFAN employees, some who moved on to other outlets, as well as others who stayed.

Jeff Smulyan, of Emmis Communications, started it all, and many of his early hires are still recognizable to this day. So many of those original employees are even better people than they are broadcasters, and that's a tall order. Folks like Jim Lampley, Eddie Coleman, Jody McDonald, John Minko, and Howie Rose gave tremendous insight, comical stories, and unforgettable history lessons on the beginning of this proud station.

Another group of people that elucidates this station's impact across 26 years on the air is the alumni, including Ian Eagle, Steve Levy, Chris Carlin, Dave Sims, Sid Rosenberg, Russ Salzberg, Kenny Albert, Kevin Burkhardt, Don La Greca, and, of course, Chris Russo and Don Imus. It was a tremendous honor for me to speak with all of them.

The current crop of talent at WFAN, on and off the air, is an eclectic mix of young and old, entertaining and bold, and New York through and through. Chernoff and Eric Spitz, the former program director who moved to CBS Sports Radio as we wrote this book, supplied great insight into the inner workings of the station, what went into some of the personnel and programming decisions, and how much work goes into the product you hear on the air daily.

The current talent was as open and honest as can be, holding nothing back for a book that uses just about everything they said. One of the great things about dealing with professional talkers is that you can ask them a question and then just let them go. Gentlemen such as Mike Francesa, Boomer Esiason, Craig Carton, Joe Benigno, Evan Roberts, Marc Malusis, Rich Ackerman, Jerry Recco, and Sweeny Murti let it all hang out, and I'm proud to say I made some new friends along the way.

Steve Somers, one of few originals who is still broadcasting on WFAN, will also never be forgotten. A proud and passionate radio professional, Steve agreed to write the foreword to this book, and I couldn't have been happier when he agreed to do so.

"Oh, stop," Somers said. "Please. It was my honor and pleasure."

Wrong, Steve. The pleasure, absolutely, was mine.

There were many executives in the sports and radio businesses who helped with research and interviews, all with a smile on their face. They include former Madison Square Garden vice president of communications Sammy Steinlight, SportsNet New York's Andrew Fegyveresi, YES Network's Eric Handler and John Filippelli, Meghan Hurlbut at the Imus Ranch, and Kevin Flaherty of HBO, among others.

I was also lucky to receive help from some other authors, including Mark Cannizzaro of the *New York Post* and Jeff Pearlman. Broadcasters from stations other than WFAN graciously allowed me to jump on their air to promote this project, including Mike Miller and Dino Costa.

In the final stages, Dan Gelston of the Associated Press was an inspiration and a terrific sounding board, while Denis Gorman was the ace of the interview playback, helping me break down response after response with efficiency and effervescence. Gorman will be an author himself soon enough.

One of the most refreshing parts of this process was talking to the listeners, the people who grew up on The Fan and remember so many key moments in the station's history. On a memorable Memorial Day weekend in 2013, the stories flowed from a faithful crew of Brooklynites—Rob and Noelle O'Shea, Matt and Christine Ferris, Anthony and Grace Gallagher, Mike Romano, and the one-of-a-kind Family Garomo: Rob, Kiersten, and JoAnn—and it was much appreciated.

Speaking of Rob O'Shea, this dedicated New York native certainly deserves a special note of recognition. Rob is a terrific friend and an unbelievable marketer. He sold more copies of *Battle on the Hudson* than you can imagine. He helped me open several new doors, and will undoubtedly do so again.

It's at times like these when you remember the people you grew up with in the real world, the friends and colleagues in and around my alma mater, Duquesne University, who always pushed me to pursue my dreams and will support my second book much like my first. I can't thank them enough: Jim Stewart, Andrew Romer, Frank Rodichok, James Orsino, Gene Pebworth, Jeff Gryboski, Gianni Floro, Garrett Jordan, Randy Stoernell, David Garth, Pete Aldrich, Troy Grunseth, John McMahon, Tom Blades, Dave Freeman, Sean Dookie, Jim Arcuri, and Mike Wattick, who keeps me going with inspirational text messages like the one that opens this section.

The crew at Triumph Books gave me my start and allowed me to build off it with this book. Without question, if it wasn't for the vision and forward thinking of Tom Bast, Noah Amstadter, and Adam Motin, this book would not be here today. They believed in this concept, they saw potential in its entirety when others didn't, and that will never be forgotten. I look forward to future projects with this team.

My family means everything to me, and to have their support made this easy. Many thanks to my mother, Kathleen Sullivan, and my sister, Anne Marie Sullivan; to Terry and Johnny Sullivan, brothers of my late father, for providing memories; to my aunt, Maureen LeLoup, for offering encouragement; and to my brother and godson, Drew Sullivan, perhaps the most loyal WFAN listener out there.

Drew lives in Virginia now, but between his computer and his mobile phone app, he is never far from The Fan. Too young to know about some of the characters in this book, I do hope this project provides him with some background on how his favorite station came together and where it goes from here. Drew lost his mother, Carol, while I wrote this in the spring of 2013, and I hope this entertains him and provides a divergence from the tough reality of the world, if only for a few days, as he moves forward with his life. Carol's sister, Joan Quinn, also provided inspiration along the way, as we all spent time together with Carol in Florida during her final days.

My rock of a wife, Amy, never let me slip when the tough times crossed our path. Waiting on an interview, stressing over a deadline, wondering how I was going to do what I was going to do and when I was going to do it—all of that happens when you're authoring a book. And Amy was always there, every step of the way, and religiously kept my focus on the end result. I will never forget her strength, determination, enthusiasm, and pride throughout this entire process. This is not a book without her.

Amy spread the word around our hometown, Fair Haven, New Jersey, when the first book came out. She pushed the message out relentlessly, and she will, without question, do so again. Fortunately for me, she could run for mayor in our town, and with the help of her friends, *Battle on the Hudson* was a hometown hit, and hopefully this book will follow suit.

And finally, my children, T.J. and Sara, who were so proud to say their father was going to be an author again. They came to the library with me to do research, they listened to some of the old WFAN clips as we reminisced, they bragged to all of their friends, they followed the book's Twitter page, and they wanted to read it before I even finished it. They are already determined readers and writers, and that makes all of this worth it. They are just beginning to discover their potential.

This book is for them and our future together.